Creative Minority

Dreams and Dilemmas

Dr. K. Sohail

Copyright

Published in 2016 by Green Zone Publishing
A division of Dr. Sohail MPC Inc.
213 Byron Street South
Whitby, Ontario Canada L1N 4P7
T. 905-666-7253 F, 905-666-4397
E-mail: welcome@drsohail.com
Website: www.drsohail.com

Sohail, K. (Khalid), 1952-
Creative Minority: Dreams and Dilemmas
K. Sohail

1. Creativity 2. Psychology
3. Psychotherapy

ISBN 978-1-927874-20-2

| Textual Design | Deana Seymore |
| Cover Design: | Shahid Shafiq |

Printed and Bound in Canada

Dedicated to…

all the Creative Children

of future generations.

Apprehension

I am afraid

The noise of the outside world

Will drown one day

The music inside

Sohail

CONTENTS

INTRODUCTION

BETTE DAVIS INTERVIEWS
DR. KHALID SOHAIL

Bette: You seem to be intrigued by Creative Personalities. What do you find special about them?

Sohail: As a poet and a psychotherapist, Creative Personalities have always fascinated me. I believe they are special people who challenge every aspect of our lives and invite us into worlds that are beyond what our ordinary eyes can see, our average hearts can feel and our traditional minds can imagine. They connect us with higher and deeper aspects of ourselves. They give us gifts of new perspectives, new insights, new points of view and new gestalts. They beautify our existence, enrich our lives and broaden our horizons. They are awesome people.

Bette: After interviewing and reading biographies of so many Creative Personalities, what do you find as a common thread in their stories?

Sohail: After reflecting upon all the stories that I have heard and read, I have concluded that Creative Personalities go through different stages in their creative journeys. In the first stage they develop a realization of the limitations of conventional methods of thinking and traditional lifestyles. They gradually become disappointed and disillusioned in themselves and their environments.

In the second stage, they discard the old ways of thinking and living, which creates a crisis in their lives. Loss of old patterns produces a conflict between Creative Personalities and the significant others in their lives. Such losses and conflicts can easily lead to a breakdown in ideals, relationships and philosophies.

In the third stage, Creative Personalities discover new ideas, new forms of expression, new lifestyles and new philosophies. They transform their breakdowns into breakthroughs. Depending upon their talents, personalities and social and political environments, Creative Personalities can become:

Scientists, who explore their world with telescopes and microscopes, using rational, logical and objective methods to discover laws of nature;

Artists, who explore the human condition aesthetically and produce poems, plays, paintings and other masterpieces of art to enrich our lives; or

Reformers and revolutionaries, who as leaders of social and political movements, push their communities to reject oppressive regimes, fight for their rights and liberties and adopt a lifestyle that respects personal freedoms and social justice. Such reformers and revolutionaries inspire communities on their historical journey of human evolution.

Whether they be scientists, artists, reformers or revolutionaries, they are always swimming against the current.

Creative Personalities are frequently put to the test by their families and communities and those tests can cost them their sanity or their lives. They may become extremely unhappy to the point of nervous breakdown, possibly ending in suicide, or they may be punished by their conservative communities who may ostracize, imprison, or even execute them.

Dr. K. Sohail

Bette: Let me move from the philosophical to personal. When did you have your first encounter with insanity?

Sohail: It was an indirect encounter. When I was about ten years old, my father, who was a scientist and taught mathematics, suffered a nervous breakdown and I witnessed the whole episode from the very beginning to the time when he fully recovered. I remember the day he was taken away from our house where I lived with my mother, father and sister to a hospital in Kohat where they tied him to a bed. Later on he was transferred to our extended family in Lahore where my mother's family nursed him at home for a few months till he fully recovered. As a ten-year-old I watched my father's illness and recovery very closely.

Bette: Were you scared of your father?

Sohail: No, I was never scared of him. He was a kind, gentle and caring father. Even during his illness he was affectionate. My aunts and uncles had told me not to enter his room, but I used to sneak in when nobody was watching. At those times he used to hug and kiss me. He never scared me.

Bette: What did he say or do that made you feel he was abnormal?

Sohail: I remember one evening when I was following him upstairs to the roof, he suddenly stopped at the top of the stairs, stared at the sky and started talking to the stars. I thought his behaviour was abnormal but it did not scare me. To me, it was innocent. Later on, I would often see him mumble and talk to himself. He used to stand in one place for hours. All those things made me aware that he was going through some unusual phase and having extra-ordinary experiences.

Bette: What was his own interpretation of his

Creative Minority: Dreams and Dilemmas

experiences?

Sohail: Friends and family members believed he had had a nervous breakdown but he believed it was a spiritual breakthrough.

Bette: What is your understanding of his encounters?

Sohail: It has remained a mystery all my life. I always wanted to unravel that mystery. Now I wonder whether those experiences unconsciously played a role in my choosing to become a psychiatrist and psychotherapist. I am aware that I was always compassionate towards mentally ill people, as I had realized that their families, like ours, needed to be supported rather than judged. I also wonder whether I have inherited creativity as well as insanity from my father's family. Alongside my father, Abdul Basit, my Uncle Arif Abdul Mateen also suffered from episodes of Depression. He was a well-known and well-respected Urdu and Punjabi poet who had been an atheist as a young man but became a mystic poet in his old age. There were others in my father's family who had Creative Personalities and also suffered from episodes of insanity. Before my father passed away I wrote a bio-fictional story about his transformation and called it *Breakthrough.*

Bette: How did your father change after his episode?

Sohail: Before that, my father had been a well-dressed man who wore three-piece suits, silk ties and polished shoes. He was proud of his higher studies in mathematics and conversed in English with his colleagues. After the episode he became a mystic. He started leading a simple and saintly life. He never again wore his suits and ties, and he grew a beard. He wore simple clothes, ate simple food and lived in simple houses. He started reading mystical books and literature. There were times I wondered if he might leave his home and family and go to some monastery in the mountains to spend the rest of his life in prayer and meditation, but he believed in serving his community. So he resigned from the college and taught high school. He was always respected by his students and their parents for his sincerity and integrity. I always felt proud of him, as he was a wise old man and a wonderful storyteller.

Bette: What was your first encounter with Creativity?
Sohail: When I was young I loved nature. I used to go for long walks in the woods where I enjoyed observing birds, animals and trees. I liked to be alone and contemplate life. Then I fell in love with words and books. The first book I read, *Life Stories of the Saints*, [*Tazkira-tul-aulia*] was from my father's library. At about age twelve I wrote an essay about my favourite female mystic, Rabia Basri, which was published in *Bachon ki Dunya*, a children's magazine. I was thrilled to see my name and essay in print—the birth of a Creative Personality. I subsequently wrote poems, short stories and essays during my student life. I was the editor of a literary magazine in Khyber Medical College in Pakistan. I have been writing and creating for the last forty years.

Bette: What was your father's reaction to your creativity?
Sohail: He used to say "You are more like your uncle than me." When he found out that I had recited a poem in a local poetry recital, he told me a story. He said, "In a village, a middle aged man, the father of three sons was sitting on the curb crying.

"'Why are you crying?' people asked him.
"'I have no son left,' he responded.

Creative Minority: Dreams and Dilemmas

"'What happened to your oldest son?'

"'He got married. Now he belongs to his wife.'

"'What about the middle son?'

"'He left his village and settled in the city. I rarely see him now.'

"'But your youngest son is neither married nor moved to the city. What happened to him?'

"'He became a poet.'"

Then my father laughed and said, "And I have only one son and he became a poet." And I had to laugh too.

Bette: How did you father's transformation affect your mother?

Sohail: It was a painful experience for her. She was a traditional person who had grown up in a traditional family. She did not know how to cope with such a major change and it caused her a lot of suffering. The more enlightened my father became, the more she regressed into chronic unhappiness. She had numerous physical and emotional problems. It became apparent to me that my father had a Creative Personality while my mother had a Traditional Personality and in spite of living in the same house, they lived in different worlds. He was idealistic while she was pragmatic.

I became aware that my father had a number of family members who had Creative Personalities. Focusing on my own parents and their families gave me the concepts of Traditional and Creative Personalities and Families that I later developed in my professional career.

Bette: As a psychotherapist in your Creative Psychotherapy Clinic you practice your Green Zone Humanistic Philosophy. What are your views about traditional psychiatry?

Sohail: As a psychotherapist I am amazed that traditional psychiatry focuses primarily on pathology and talks about schizoid, hysterical, psychopathic and many other personality disorders. In the textbooks of psychiatry there are no discussions on love and creativity. Unfortunately traditional psychiatrists do not discuss Creative Personalities and their dilemmas living with Traditional families and communities. Developing these concepts has helped me greatly in my clinical practice.

In my clinic I have worked with many Creative Teenagers and Creative Adults who suffered from emotional problems and experienced nervous breakdowns. In therapy I helped them accept their unique personality and discover cooperative and harmonious rather than angry and confrontative relationships with their families and communities. It was sad that many Creative Personalities that I saw in my practice had been diagnosed by traditional therapists and mental health professionals as suffering from psychopathic, hysterical, narcissistic and socio-pathic personalities. Some Creative Personalities might share some of the characteristics with these personality disorders but the differences outweigh the similarities. In this book I have devoted a few chapters to psychotherapy with Creative Personalities.

Bette: Who do you think will benefit from your book?
Sohail: I am hopeful that it will help many people. First of all it will help Creative Personalities whether scientists or artists, philosophers or writers, reformers or revolutionaries, to understand themselves better and deal with their dilemmas and dreams in a constructive way by recognizing the dark side of creativity and the bright side of insanity. I think it is

Creative Minority: Dreams and Dilemmas

important for them to recognize that by obtaining family support and professional help they can transform a breakdown into a breakthrough. I think this book will help build a bridge between artists and psychotherapists. This book will also help traditional psychiatrists and psychotherapists to pay special attention to the special needs of Creative Personalities and think twice before prescribing medications and offering traditional therapy. Hopefully this book will also help traditional parents and teachers to recognize the special needs of Creative Children who struggle with authority figures, so that they can develop a cooperative rather than a confrontative attitude and relationship. I am also hopeful that this book will break down walls between different disciplines and build bridges between different traditions, philosophies and cultures, so that we can all work together to decrease human suffering and support creativity so that people can grow to their fullest and serve humanity to the best of their ability. I believe we need supportive families and communities so that Creative Personalities can evolve and grow and create, as it is a matter of life and death not only for individuals but also for communities and cultures. I believe the future of any community and culture depends upon how the traditional majority deals with their creative minority. In the words of the historian Arnold Toynbee, "To give a fair chance to potential creativity is a matter of life and death of any society. This is all important because the outstanding creative ability of a small percentage of the population is mankind's ultimate capital asset…."

Dr. K. Sohail

Creative Minority: Dreams and Dilemmas

Dr. K. Sohail

Part One

Creativity

CHAPTER ONE

ENCOUNTERS WITH CREATIVE PERSONALITIES

When I reminisce about my literary life, I realize that alongside creating and publishing books, some of the most exciting experiences of my adult life have been meeting Creative Personalities from different artistic and cultural backgrounds. Some of them I met only once and interviewed them for creative projects and books, while others became close friends. Among the Creative Personalities I was fortunate to meet were poets, short story writers, actors, musicians, journalists, philosophers, scientists, and political activists. Some lived locally so I could see them frequently, while others I met during my travels in Asia, the Middle East, Europe, North America and South Africa.

All these Creative People had unique personalities and lifestyles. Interestingly, the same people I found fascinating had been frustrating for their family, friends and communities. I found their idiosyncrasies and eccentricities amusing rather than irritating. I learnt more about human psychology from them than from psychiatric textbooks, as they had unique insights about life and the human condition and their dialogues were full of wisdom. I found them not only entertaining but also enlightening. I was always fascinated and interested in their personalities, as I believe that creators can be as complex and mysterious as their creations. Creative Personalities have remained an ongoing source of inspiration for my literary, psychological and philosophical journeys.

Reflecting on those personalities and my encounters with them, I ask myself how these Creative Personalities are different from my other sincere but traditional friends, and a profile of their personalities and lifestyles appears in my mind. I am aware that this profile of the Creative Personality is not based on any scientific study; however, I have had a rare opportunity to share these people's lives in an emotionally intimate way and peep into the corners of their worlds that were hidden from their neighbors and colleagues, even family members. Many of them shared some very private aspects of their lives in their interviews with me.

I remember the evening when I interviewed Dr. Gopi Chand Narang. After the interview I confessed that in spite of conducting dozens of interviews with other writers I was a bit nervous because he was a winner of numerous awards and a famous critic. Listening to my confession Dr. Narang smiled and shared that he too was nervous. He said that he had been interviewed by many journalists but never by a psychiatrist. After Dr. Narang's interview was published in a magazine in India, he sent me a copy and told me that he had received complimentary letters from all over the world from people who were impressed that he had shared aspects of his life in that interview that he had never before disclosed. Dr. Narang graciously gave me some of that credit by stating that I had asked him the right questions. We all know that to get the right answers one needs to ask the right questions. Not only Dr. Narang but many other Creative Personalities confessed that they shared more of themselves with me than they had done with other interviewers. Maybe my being a psychotherapist made them feel comfortable and helped me pursue intimate dialogues about their philosophies and lifestyles.

Reminiscing about the interviews that I conducted over the years and thinking about the intimate dialogues I had with Creative Personalities about their lives and philosophies, I have come to the conclusion that Creative Personalities are made of different clay than their contemporaries. They continue their journey on a road less travelled.

Based on my encounters and interviews with Creative Personalities I have drawn some impressions and inferences about their personalities and lifestyles. As a student of human psychology I have always had a keen interest in the mysteries of the Creative Personality. Although each Creative Personality is unique, I feel that as a group they have some characteristics that distinguish them from traditional people. Some of them have more of these characteristics than others.

1. CREATIVE PERSONALITIES ARE
HIGHLY SENSITIVE TO THEIR ENVIRONMENTS

One of the foremost characteristics that I have observed in Creative Personalities is that they are highly sensitive to their environments, physical as well as emotional, social as well as cultural. They can easily laugh and cry and can make others laugh and cry as well. Some do it in person while others do it through their creative works like poems or plays or paintings. Creative Personalities have such an unusual relationship with emotions that I feel as if they have a special heart or have many hearts, as they seem to relate to life on a different wavelength

Creative Minority: Dreams and Dilemmas

than others around them, or on many wavelengths at the same time. They tune in to aspects of life of which others are unaware. It comes naturally to them to empathize with other people's experiences and then express their encounters in their creative projects. They become creative and cultural ambassadors of their communities. Unfortunately the heightened emotional sensitivity of Creative Personalities can be a mixed blessing. It can generate a lot of excitement and happiness but can also cause much hurt and pain. It can be a blessing for their art but a curse in their personal lives. It helps them empathize with others and create masterpieces but it also causes sleepless nights.

Many Creative Personalities have confessed to me that they were highly sensitive for as long as they could remember, even as children. Their own Creative Children often present the same sensitivity.

Many psychologists and parents have observed that Creative Children tend to be more sensitive to physical and emotional stimuli than average children. Parents who have more than one child can easily differentiate between a Creative and a non-Creative Child. Whether it is the temperature of the milk or the volume of noise, these children react strongly. They are easily startled by strange noises or get upset if the milk is not just the right temperature. Many parents find them temperamental and difficult to parent.

Creative Children also react more strongly to the changing moods of their parents. The same parents who have a stable relationship with their other children have a stormy relationship with the Creative Child and a difficult time adjusting to the roller coaster nature of their relationship. They feel as though they are fighting a losing battle. It is not uncommon for parents of an only child who is creative to feel guilty and inadequate.

Creative Children are difficult to take care of as they

are challenging from an early age. It is amusing for me to watch my creative friends react differently to their Creative Children than do their traditional spouses. The same Creative Children who are quite frustrating for traditional parents become a source of amusement and excitement for Creative Parents as they can identify with them, realizing that they had been like them when they were small themselves.

2. CREATIVE PERSONALITIES LIKE THEIR SOLITUDE

People who create are well aware that the creative process is a private and solitary experience. Thus Creative Personalities like to be alone for extended periods of time to nurture their creativity. The same solitude they enjoy, others dread. Creative Personalities could be alone without feeling lonely. It is during this solitude that Creative Personalities get in touch with their inner selves, their higher and deeper selves, their unconscious states of mind and their secret reservoirs of creative energy. It is during those silences that they connect with their muse and receive their creative gifts. Creative Personalities have a difficult time nurturing their creativity when they are busy with their routine jobs, families and day-to-day responsibilities. They want time to be idle and lazy, and do nothing, so that they have ample time to think, daydream, fantasize and create. The freedom of time provides an opportunity for their Creative Selves to leave the shore of rationality and delve deeper into the depths of the ocean of unconscious, finally returning with new insights and new forms of expression. Creative Personalities can be compared to fishermen who patiently wait on the shore to catch a fish. The same hours that look lazy to others are full of creative potential. They look forward to weekends and holidays, when they are not involved in the routine of work, to complete their creative projects. It is a time when they can play with new ideas, concepts and images.

Solitary moments are very valuable for Creative Personalities as they provide an opportunity to daydream. Nobel Laureate Isaac Bashevis Singer who created wonderful stories and fascinating characters stated, "One might anticipate that persons engaging in frequent day dreaming would be characterized by a considerable exploratory tendency, at least at an ideational level, and perhaps by creativity in their story telling abilities." So it is not uncommon for Creative Personalities to interrupt their routine work on a regular basis so that they can indulge in free spirited daydreaming and nurture their creativity. It is also not unusual for their dear ones to accuse them of being lazy rather than creative, as they cannot differentiate between the visible and the invisible labor of Creative Personalities.

Many Creative Personalities have a favorite place where they feel most inspired and creative. Scientists have their laboratories, artists their studios, poets their long walks in the woods and mystics their monasteries. Virginia Woolf used to suggest that creative women have "a room of one's own." That room is physical as well as metaphorical, a safe place where Creative Personalities can be alone and meet their muse privately.

It is not uncommon for the spouses and family members of Creative Personalities to feel ignored when Creative Personalities withdraw to their private worlds. The more insecure the friends and relatives, the more they tend to accuse Creative Personalities of being self-centered and narcissistic. Many Creative Personalities have a difficult time explaining to their

dear ones that they are not rejecting them, they just
have a need to be alone, daydream and create.

3. CREATIVE PERSONALITIES ARE IN LOVE
WITH THE MEDIUM OF THEIR EXPRESSION

Creative Personalities are fascinated with the medium
of their expression, be it words or colors, sounds or
fragrances, concepts or ideologies, psychological or
sociological phenomena. From an early age they were
intrigued and mystified by those media and loved to
play with them. Although it started as play, gradually
they realized that they could create some novel and
original products.

I met a number of poets, writers, artists and
philosophers who spend countless hours exploring
and enjoying new developments in their area of
interest. The same words and sounds that are ordinary
for others take on a new fascination for these Creative
Personalities as they are always exploring new
possibilities and dimensions in old patterns. They
experiment with new forms which become more
beautiful and meaningful for them. I sometimes
wonder how much time the author had to spend to
construct the following sentence: "There is more self
love than love in jealousy."

Most people do not realize how much time and
energy have been invested in a creative product like a
poem, a play or a painting. Works of art are gifts of
love from the artist to others and those gifts are
created because those Creative Personalities are in
love with the medium they use to create their
masterpieces.

4. CREATIVE PERSONALITIES STRUGGLE
WITH DISCIPLINE

Although it starts as play, Creative Personalities

become aware at an early age that life has offered them a special gift in the form of creative energy and potential, and if they can focus their energy and give it shape they can create an original creative product. Alongside that realization they also become aware that to create a wonderful product they have to learn the craft that is part of the art.

Some Creative Personalities are fortunate to have a parent, a relative or a teacher who recognizes their creative potential and nurtures their talent by not only providing emotional and financial support but also instilling patience and discipline so that the creative energies and inspirations find a focus. Many fine arts schools try to provide that guidance and structure.

From intimate discussions with artists and writers, I became aware that some forms of art are more demanding than others. Writing a novel demands more discipline than creating a short story, which in turn requires more discipline than producing a poem. In some forms of creative expression the artist depends more on inspiration while in others there is far more perspiration. I met one novelist who had prepared six different manuscripts of six hundred pages before he felt satisfied that the finished product.

In my book *Literary Encounters* I compared the dilemmas of poets, short story writers and novelists: "While I was listening to different writers share their experiences of creating literature, I realized that those experiences were not only reflections of their creative personalities, but also the type of creative work in which they were involved. Those experiences varied depending upon whether the writer was creating poetry, short stories or novels. They reminded me of my late grandmother who used to tell me that there were three ways of getting water in a village. Some people preferred to obtain water from well; they dug

Dr. K. Sohail

in the ground in their backyards for weeks or months to reach the desired depth to find water. Sometimes they had to dig deeper to find pure water and each time they needed water they had to throw the bucket into the well and then pull it out. Others did not want to work that hard for that long but they were willing to carry the bucket for a few miles to the nearest river and bring the water back. The third group consisted of those who relied on rain. They did not have to work hard but they did have to wait. They had no control over the weather. Sometimes it did not rain for months, while at other times it not only rained, it poured. To me, poets seem like artists who wait for the rain, short story writers go to the river, while novelists dig wells in the backyard.

I have met many talented writers and artists who lack discipline. I have witnessed many of their creative projects started but never completed. It seemed as though they had a series of creative miscarriages.

5. CREATIVE PERSONALITIES ARE FASCINATED WITH ABSTRACTION

It has been my experience that Creative Personalities like to communicate in an indirect way. They find direct communication too ordinary and concrete. They like to use words, sounds and colors in a creative way, so they are fascinated with symbols and metaphors. However, the more symbolic and metaphorical the communication the artist or writer uses, the greater the danger of miscommunication. Such communication is a mixed blessing. On the one hand, it can have multiple layers of meanings and be a source of great entertainment and enlightenment for artists, critics and intellectuals; but it can also be beyond comprehension for those who have not developed a refined taste in art and literature. We all know that some families and communities are more culturally and creatively evolved than others.

Over the years I have met two groups of Creative Personalities. The first group believes in creative communication with their readers, viewers and listeners, while the second group is so preoccupied with the perfection of their own creative and artistic expression that they give little importance to the realities of effective communication. Some Creative Personalities choose to follow the masses while others are determined to lead them. Some produce popular literature while others create serious works. Those who produce serious literature may have to wait for years, even decades, before their creations are widely recognized. Artists like Vincent Van Gogh and writers like Franz Kafka were acknowledged, appreciated and admired far more after their death than during their lives. They were far ahead of their times. During their era they were considered confusing and surrealistic.

6. CREATIVE PERSONALITIES
CHALLENGE TRADITIONS

Creative Personalities face the challenge of being misunderstood, not only by the masses but also by contemporary artists, writers and critics. The more non-traditional the artist, the greater is the likelihood of their challenging the artistic traditions. It is not uncommon for traditional critics to judge harshly any new form of expression. We all know that traditional poets and critics took a long time before they could accept, acknowledge, respect and appreciate blank verse and prose poetry. The unacceptable of one generation can be the respected of the next. The trails of one generation can be the highways for those who come later. Alongside experimenting with artistic traditions, Creative Personalities also challenge the ethical and moral norms of their families and communities. People react to their creations, sometimes very strongly. When Creative Personalities challenge the conservative social traditions of their families and communities, they can expect harsh and reactionary judgments from political organizations and religious institutions.

We are all aware that the creations of James Joyce and Henry Miller were banned for a long time before they received the blessings of their communities. In some cases writers and artists like Saadat Hasan Minto and Oscar Wilde were forced to defend themselves in court against charges of pornography. Those who challenged religious traditions were charged with blasphemy and had to make sacrifices for their values and ideals.

7. CREATIVE PERSONALITIES ARE QUITE PASSIONATE

Many Creative Personalities that I have met in my life were very passionate—they displayed a certain intensity in their interactions with their environments. Some of them showed that intensity in their creative products while others manifested it in their personalities as well. It seemed as though they had a strong *antigenic* quality in their attitudes that produced *antibodies* in others when there was a creative and emotional exchange. Such an *antigen /antibody* reaction became fertile ground for a confrontative exchange. As time passed the conflict escalated and over the years many of these Creative Personalities developed a tumultuous relationship with their communities and visa versa. Some are loved, while others are hated; and some are loved and hated with the same passion simultaneously. It is not uncommon for Creative

Personalities to face penalties, punishments and persecutions from traditional families, conservative political organizations and fundamentalist religious institutions. Such judgments force some writers and artists to use pseudonyms or go into exile, as they are afraid of being jailed or executed.

8. CREATIVE PERSONALITIES CAN BE DIFFICULT TO LIVE WITH

Creative Personalities might be very charming and exciting from a distance but they are usually difficult people to live with because of their idiosyncratic behaviors and eccentric lifestyles. I have met many parents of creative teenagers and spouses of creative adults who told me that it was easy to love them but hard to live with them. The more obsessive and perfectionistic their personalities and the higher their expectations from themselves and others, the more disappointed they were in the Creative Personalities. It has been my personal and professional observation that in day-to-day living there are generally four areas of conflict that create tension for the families:

A. Cleanliness: There are many creative teenagers and adults who have no sense of cleanliness. Their rooms remain unclean and work places disorganized. Such sloppy habits of creative people can become a source of frustration for people around them.

B. Time: Creative people usually ignore time. Many do not even wear watches. They are usually late, even forgetful and their dear ones spend hours and hours waiting for them. Many parents of creative teenagers wish their children had better time management. What people consider careless, creative people consider carefree, what others perceive as irresponsible, creative people perceive as free spirited, and what others call impulsive creative people call spontaneous. Not surprisingly, there are ongoing conflicts between creative people and their friends and relatives.

C. Money: Most creative teenagers I met had no sense of money management—they spent freely and were seldom concerned about earning. When they reached adulthood, they had poor money management skills. It was not uncommon for them to be in debt to complete their creative projects. Those projects were pursued to fulfill their dreams rather than generate money. The creative people who were financially successful were those who had the support of financially responsible secretaries, assistants and managers.

D. Morality: Most creative people I encountered disagreed with the moral standards of their families and communities. They generally followed their hearts and did not feel obliged to comply with the community's religious and social traditions, which often resulted in conflict with the members of traditional organizations and religious institutions.

9. CREATIVE PERSONALITIES DESTROY BEFORE THEY CREATE

While reviewing the interviews and life stories of Creative Personalities I realized that they had a special relationship with destructiveness as a part of the creative journey which became a source of great concern for their dear ones.

One such example was Charles Darwin. From an early age Darwin was passionate about collecting specimens. Even as a teenager, he had a large collection of dead birds and animals. At one stage his family became concerned about Darwin's obsession with killing animals. They interpreted it as delinquency and feared that he might become a psychopath. Their criticism made him feel guilty. They did not appreciate that he was collecting specimens for his research and not getting some perverse, sadistic pleasure.

I find it intriguing how destructiveness is intimately connected with creativity; I think that it is unfair to judge the behaviors of creative people until we ascertain their intentions. It is not uncommon for families and communities to penalize and persecute Creative Personalities because of a lack of understanding and appreciation of their underlying intentions and passions.

It is important to differentiate between the destructiveness of Creative Personalities in which it is a controlled, means to an end, and the destructiveness of psychopaths who have no conscience, to whom it is an end in itself because they experience a perverse pleasure from hurting others.

Some Creative Personalities who cannot cope with stress have breakdowns of a psychotic or psychopathic nature which can be expressed in the form of destructive behavior.

10. CREATIVE PERSONALITIES EXPERIENCE UNIQUE FRUSTRATIONS AND CONFLICTS

Since many Creative Personalities challenge traditions and authority, they are often seen as delinquent and judged harshly. Such confrontative relationships cause them much frustration.

Some creative people become angry and resentful and experience emotional and social breakdowns, while others find their frustrations an ongoing source of inspiration. They consider all their experiences as raw material for their masterpieces. Creative

Personalities can tend to be particularly sensitive to human suffering because of having experienced certain tragedies in their own lives, such as the loss of a parent when very young or physical illnesses or emotional problems as an adult. Their own suffering helps them develop a humanistic attitude as well as empathy for the sufferings of others. Such empathy inspires them to become involved in activities and organizations that work to alleviate the suffering of other human beings.

11. CREATIVE PEOPLE ARE FASCINATED WITH THE MYSTERIES OF NATURE

Creative Personalities are intrigued with the mysteries of life. Such a fascination also adds a mysterious dimension to their personalities. They are interested in understanding phenomena that others take for granted. Scientists strive to discover the laws of nature with microscopes and telescopes while artists, writers and philosophers explore the mysteries of the human condition. Creative Personalities retain a childlike innocence throughout their lives. They are always in search of truth, whether it is personal truth or social truth, national truth or global truth. Their truth helps them create masterpieces at a personal level along with just and enlightened communities at a social level.

12. CREATIVE PERSONALITIES HAVE A PHILOSOPHY OF ART AND LIFE

When I review my interviews of creative people and the biographies I studied, I realized that creative people have a philosophy of their creative work and life. Some believe in art for art's sake. Like Oscar Wilde, they believe that art has its own integrity and independent aesthetic values. It does not have to serve any other purpose. On the other hand there are artists who believe that art should serve life and must be intimately connected with social and political issues, to help the masses to understand and improve their quality of life. There are still others who believe that genuine art embraces aesthetic as well as humanistic values. It is beautiful as well as meaningful, entertaining as well as enlightening.

Creative people who get involved in the process of social change can be divided into two groups. Some believe in peaceful evolution, while others in violent revolution. Some are followers of Leo Tolstoy and Martin Luther King, Jr. while others are fascinated by Vladimir Lenin, Mao Tse Tung and Che Guevara. All their lives they produce creative products, which are not poems and paintings, but rather reforms and revolutions. I have discussed the personalities and philosophies of 20th century reformers and revolutionaries in my book *Prophets of Violence, Prophets of Peace.*

In essence Creative Personalities are dreamers. They want their communities to live more meaningful lives. They believe that the better we understand the mysteries of nature and human beings, the more we will be able to grow and evolve. All these efforts have created sciences, arts and philosophies that each generation inherits from previous generations and passes on to the next. Creative Personalities hope that we leave the world in better shape than that which we inherited from our ancestors. They dream of better tomorrows. They want our grandchildren to have more enjoyable and enlightened lives than those of our grandparents.

Creative Personalities are as fascinating as their creations and that they play a significant role in making our lives more entertaining and enlightening. I believe we owe a lot to these gifted people. I feel fortunate to have known many of them personally and to have read the biographies of many more - they are a great source of inspiration. Families, schools and communities need to recognize Creative Children at an early age so that their creativity can be nurtured. I hope that rather than judging Creative Personalities with our traditional and conservative methods and systems, we can support and appreciate their unique personalities and extra-ordinary contributions, which in turn will enrich our lives.

CHAPTER TWO

CREATIVE PERSONALITIES AND THEIR SPECIAL GIFTS

Creative Personalities are special people because they are born with special gifts, the gifts of creativity. These offerings however are present in the form of potential and raw material and need to be nurtured and nourished for them to mature.

Psychologists and psychiatrists have attempted to unravel the mysteries of the creative process, to discover how Creative Personalities are different than traditional personalities around them and to determine the most significant characteristics of their special gifts. Because of their creative imaginations, creative people are able to conceive innovative ideas, nurture them, develop them and then deliver them in the form of creative products - their masterpieces. For many psychologists creativity has been a difficult concept to define, as it is a multi-faceted and multi-dimensional phenomenon. Experts have identified different facets and dimensions of this mysterious process.

Carl Rogers wrote "... there must be something observable, some product of creation. Though my fantasies may be extremely novel, they cannot usefully be defined as creative unless they eventuate in some observable product ... unless they are symbolized in words, or written in a poem or translated into a work of art or fashioned into an invention." (Ref. 2)

Phyllis Greenacre stated, "I use the term creativity ... to mean, the capacity for or activity of making something new, original or inventive, no matter in what field. It is not merely the making of a product, even a good product, but of one which has the characteristic of originality." (Ref. 3)

Rollo May broadened the horizons of creativity, saying, "Creativity is a yearning for immortality ... creativity is not merely the innocent spontaneity of our youth and childhood, it must also be married to the passion of the adult human being, which is a passion to live beyond one's death." (Ref. 11)

THEORIES
Experts in many fields have put forward a number of different theories highlighting various aspects and dimensions of the creative process. Some of these theories are descriptive while others are dynamic.

Four Stages
In 1926 Joseph Wallace presented one of the most popular theories, which held that the creative process consists of four stages: Preparation, Incubation, Illumination, and Verification. (Ref. 1)

Catherine Patrick in her book *What is Creative Thinking?* discusses those stages in detail. She states that during the "Preparation" stage the Creative Person aims to acquire more information about the problem than he already possesses. During "Incubation" there is recurrence of the chief idea, which is finally adopted as the solution to a problem, or the subject of art in the stage of Illumination. The stage of "Illumination" consists of "a sudden intuition or a clear insight or a feeling ... something between a 'hunch' and a 'solution' and at other times the result of 'sustained effort'." (Ref. 4) This stage has also been known in literature as the Eureka experience when the Creative Person says to himself, "This is IT! This is what I wanted to express." The final stage is "Verification" in which the essential idea or outline which appeared in the Illumination stage is revised or verified; if verification is not possible, then the outline is revisited, so that "Revision" can occur simultaneously with the stage of "Verification". Patrick noted, "The four stages may overlap, as Incubation may appear during Preparation and Revision may begin during the Illumination stage." (Ref. 4)

Primary, Secondary, Tertiary Process Thinking

A number of other theorists who belong to the psychoanalytical school of thinking look at the creative process from a totally different perspective which they call Primary, Secondary and Tertiary Process thinking.

Human minds are capable of two kinds of thinking: Secondary Process and Primary Process thinking. Secondary Process thinking is logical, rational and objective, and is used in problem-solving. While, Primary Process thinking is subjective and is related to the emotional life. People use it in their dreams and in humour. Children start their lives with Primary Process thinking and gradually learn Secondary Process thinking as they grow older.

Freud tried to explain creativity from an analytical point of view. He compared literary work to fantasies and daydreaming, which are related to fulfilment of wishes and Primary Process thinking. He also "saw a great similarity between neurosis and creativity; they both originate in conflicts which spring from more fundamental biological drives. In other words, they are attempts to solve conflicts that originate in the powerful human instincts." (Ref. 1)

Freud seemed to be preoccupied with biological drives, instincts and Primary Process thinking. Other psychologists and psychiatrists believe that in creativity the Primary Process thinking joins with Secondary Process thinking, which deals with reality in a logical and rational way and they form a synthesis. Silvano Arieti named this synthesis Tertiary Process thinking, while Pinchas Noy compared it with insight

When these new inter-categorical schemata are produced in a creative mind and result in the highest art forms, it is always because the self centered and the reality oriented categories have been integrated into one new entity. Thus by integrating abstract concepts and concrete images, objective information and subjective states of experiencing ideas and emotions, wishes and reality considerations, the artist succeeds in achieving the ultimate aim of any creative art: to weave into a single tapestry the warp and weft of self and reality ... neither creativity nor insight can ever be achieved by either the self-centered primary process or the reality-oriented secondary process alone, but only by a kind of cognitive based on a synthesis of the operational modes of both processes. (Ref. 6)

Psychoanalyst and art historian Ernst Kris conceptualised the creative process within his own frame of orientation: on one hand he considered that the use of Primary Process in creativity was "a regression in the service of ego", and on the other hand he felt that some part of creativity may be the function of the conflict-free area of ego, the

Dr. K. Sohail

autonomous ego. He believed that "creative imagination may lead to concrete achievements, some of them art, others devoted mainly and solely to problem solving; to inventiveness in science or simply to the enrichment of an individual's existence." (Ref. 1)

Personal and Collective Unconscious
Carl Jung wrote about creativity focusing on the aesthetic process. He believed that the creative process has two modes, the psychological and the visionary. The psychological mode is related to human experience and consciousness while the visionary mode deals with the deeper part of the human personality, the timeless depth, and the "collective unconscious." He felt that the latter, the repository of ancestral experience shared by all human beings, expresses itself through symbols and images.

Phyllis Greenacre also made significant contributions towards understanding the creative process and the personality of the artist. She suggested that the ego of the future artist is capable of dissociating itself from real objects and thus developing a "love affair with the world." In this connection she talks about the "collective audience" and "collective alternates." She wrote, "In an effort to clarify this in my mind I have adopted the phrase *collective alternatives* to describe this range of extended experience which may surround or become attached to the main focus of object relationships: ... the true artist may be more faithful with deeper inner integrity in his relation to his collective audience than he is with his personal connections." (Ref. 1)

Alfred Adler explained creativity with his Compensatory Theory of Creativity, stating, "human beings produce art, science and other aspects of culture to compensate for their own inadequacies."

(Ref. 11)

These descriptions clearly capture how the creative process makes a bond between the inner and the outer worlds of the artist and the writer.

Four Characteristics

Research scholars who have seriously and methodically studied the creative process have presented four characteristics of creative thinking: Divergent, Synectic, Janusian, and Homospatial.

In our day-to-day problem solving activities, we use convergent thinking when selecting one correct answer from a number of choices. When you ask someone what is common to oranges, apples, bananas and mangoes, he uses convergent thinking when he answers, "They are all fruits." On the other hand when you ask someone how many things he can make with a circle, he uses imagination or divergent thinking to answer, "Face, clock, wheel, ball and orange." (Ref. 12)

Educational psychologists notice that when children enter school their capacity for divergent or imaginative thinking is quite high. But by the time they graduate as teenagers they have learned logical, rational, problem-solving convergent thinking to pass their exams and in the process have lost their capacity for divergent thinking. Most psychology tests when assessing intelligence focus mainly on convergent thinking. Some psychologists who have a keen interest in creativity are devising tests to assess divergent thinking.

W.J. Gordon in 1961 expressed the view that creative thinking uses synectics (a Greek word meaning joining together of diverse elements) which is composed of two basic operations, "Making the strange familiar" and "Making the familiar strange." Gordon believed that creative people can see similarities between dissimilar things and also see old things in a fresh new way. They can look at the same thing, person, problem or system in many different ways, and develop fresh insights. (Ref. 12)

Albert Rothenberg described Janusian Cognition and Homospatial Process as significant elements of the creative process. In Janusian Cognition, "multiple opposites or antitheses" are conceived simultaneously and in Homospatial Process, two or more discrete entities are conceived as occupying the same space. Such processes reflect the originality and vivid imagination of creative minds and lead to new identities. Such thinking involves abstraction and gives birth to metaphors used frequently in poetry. (Ref. 16) Writers use the language in such a way that the same words can suggest multiple meanings. Jean Paul Sartre once said in an interview, "What distinguishes literature from scientific communication, for example, is that literature is ambiguous. The artist of language arranges words in such a way that, depending on how he emphasizes them or gives weight to them, they will have one meaning, and another, and yet another, each time at different levels." (Ref. 17)

Hierarchy of Creative Process
Irving Taylor in 1959 suggested a hierarchy of creative process depending upon the aesthetic and societal value of the product. He named the stages Expressive, Productive, Inventive, Innovative and Emergentive. Expressive creations are the spontaneous drawings of children. Productive creations are the works of art in which artists have mastered the technique and the craft. In Inventive, Innovative and Emergentive thinking, scientists, artists, mystics, philosophers, reformers and revolutionaries can come up with such profound insights or forms that they change the way

human beings see themselves and the world around them. (Ref. 12)

The wisdom of Confucius, Buddha and Socrates, the scientific discoveries of Darwin and Einstein, the art of Pablo Picasso and Vincent Van Gogh, the reforms of Mohandas Gandhi and Martin Luther King, Jr., and the revolutions of Che Guevara and Nelson Mandela can be seen as examples of those profound creations. I have discussed the psychology, philosophy and personalities of reformers and revolutionaries in my earlier book *Prophets of Violence, Prophets of Peace.*

REFERENCES:

1. Silvano. A., *Creativity - The Magic Synthesis* New York:
 Basic Books 1985

2. Rogers, C., *On Becoming a Person* Boston: Houghton,
 Mifflin, 1982.

3. Greenacre, P., *Play In Relation To Creative Imagination,*
 Sophia Mirriss Memorial Lecture, San Francisco,
 California, March 2, 1959.

4. Patrick, C., *What Is Creative Thinking* New York:
 Philosophical Library, 1972.

5. Hutchinson, D., "*Varieties of Insight in Humans*",
 Psychiatry, 2: 323-332, 1939.

6. Noy, P., *Insight and Creativity,* Presented Sept. 1976,
 New York, Psychoanalytic Society.

7. Greenacre, P., *The Childhood Of The Artist (Libidinal
 Phase Development & Giftedness),* Paper panel
 discussion, American Psychoanalytic
 Association, New York, Dec. 1956.

8. Kretschmer, *The Psychology Of Men of Genius,*
 University of Marburg, 1951.

9. Hutchinson, D., *The Period Of Frustration In Creative
 Endeavour,* New York: Basic Books Inc., 1969.

10. Arieti, S., *Interpretation of Schizophrenia.* New York:
 Basic Books Inc. Publishers, 1974.

11. May, R., *The Courage To Create,* New York: Bantam

Books, 1981.

12. Tyson, M., and F., Brian, E. *New Horizons In Psychology*. England: Penguin Books, 1966.

13. Steinberg, R., *Wisdom*. New York: Cambridge University, Press, 1990.

14. Nin, A., *The Journals Of Anais Nin*. New York: Quartet, Books, 1977.

15. Freud, S., *The Interpretation Of Dreams*, USA: Gryphon Editions Inc., 1988.

16. Rothenberg, A., *Creativity and Madness*, New York: John, Hopkins University Press, 1990

17. Sartre, J., *Life/Situations - Essays Written and Spoken*, Canada: Random House, 1977

18. Campbell, J., *The Portable Jung*, New York: Penguin Books, 1971.

19. Sohail, K. *Literary Encounters*, Pakistan: Gora Publishers, 1992.

20. Shephard, A., *Aesthetics*. England: Oxford University Press, 1987.

CHAPTER THREE

CREATIVE PRODUCTS

The artist, Marc Chagall called artistic products "the children of the soul" for which artists experience labour pains the same way mothers do to deliver babies. It is easy to recognize human babies and assess whether they are alive and healthy and strong, but to evaluate the artistic qualities and meaningfulness of creative products is very difficult. Over the centuries, numerous philosophers, artists and critics have expressed their views about the qualities and value of creative products.

When some philosophers saw artists sitting in their studios drawing still objects and portraits of people, or standing in front of their easels outdoors painting mountains, valleys or trees, they felt that these artists were merely imitating nature. Plato criticized artists for imitating natural objects which he believed were themselves imitations of the objects, which existed in God's mind. Other artists objected to this notion and highlighted that artists draw what they see with their inner eye using their imagination rather than what they see with their naked eye. Michelangelo expressed his ideas of trying to paint and sculpt an ideal form because he believed that beauty "carries the eye up to those heights which I am preparing here to paint and sculpt."

Visual arts may be accused of mere imitations but when we read a novel, attend a stage play or watch a movie, we enter the domain of representation. Artists try to represent certain aspects of social realities. In creating novels and screenplays writers create a fictional reality, which might be based on but still is independent from social reality and a sophisticated reader and viewer knows the difference. While the viewer may feel sad that a character died on the stage he also knows that the same character will play the same role the next day on the same stage. By creating fictional realities the artists not only use their own imagination but also stimulate the imagination of their readers and viewers.

Genuine art touches us at an emotional level. Wordsworth wrote, "All good poetry is a spontaneous flow of powerful emotions" and according to Tolstoy, "art is the contagion of feeling." Poets and artists, rather than sharing ideas and concepts like scientists and philosophers, focus on feelings. They seek to touch our hearts and souls rather than our brains. They want their audience to develop an empathy with the characters and their conflicts, rather than simply experiencing an intellectual understanding of the situation. Genuine artists, rather than stating their feelings directly, try to find indirect and subtle ways to express themselves, whether through colours or sounds or symbols or metaphors which they find a more effective and creative way to communicate with their audience.

Artistic products not only play a role as the creative expressions of the artist but are also the bridges of communication. A sophisticated artist needs a sophisticated viewer or listener or reader. Thus, in any community the number of people who can enjoy opera, abstract art and steam-of consciousness novels are relatively few.

There is always an ongoing dialogue between artists and the public. Some artists aim for commercial success and popularity and want their books to become bestsellers even if they have to sacrifice their morals and integrity, while others follow their inner voices. They follow their own hearts and create only when they are

Dr. K. Sohail

inspired. Such artists are less affected by financial rewards, public opinion or the views of the critics. An unfortunate consequence of this attitude is that they may have to sacrifice and struggle all their lives, especially if they depend on their art for their livelihood. Many artists have suffered when their novels or movies were banned because they challenged the moral, religious and ethical norms and traditions of society or were disliked by the people in power. Writings of James Joyce and Henry Miller were banned for a quarter of a century before they could be sold publicly.

Genuine artists share their personal truths and hope that by touching the hearts, minds and souls of their audience, they can collectively discover their subjective and objective truths. They believe that art helps us to become better human beings and plays a role in the journey of human evolution. Artists believe that stimulating one's imagination enriches our life aesthetically. Anne Shephard ends her book *Aesthetics* by stating, "Art engages both the emotions and the intellect and the study of art requires a combination of imaginative flexibility and intellectual discipline. If we develop our ability to respond to art we shall develop our potential as human beings." (Ref. 1, p. 50)

CHAPTER FOUR

CREATIVE CHILDREN, TRADITIONAL FAMILIES AND SCHOOLS

Studying the biographies of Creative Personalities, I became aware that many of them had great difficulties coping with the traditional families and school systems in their childhood. Creative Children, because of their unconventional thinking and nontraditional attitude felt quite frustrated with the institutional setting of the schools. They longed for an environment where they could be spontaneous, express their creativity and explore their potential. They felt suffocated in the traditional systems. The more controlling and regimented the schools, the more they felt their wings being clipped. Some of those Creative Children endured and tolerated their restrictive environments while others challenged the authorities and rebelled; and in many cases they subsequently rejected and or were expelled from those institutions, or withdrew into their own private worlds to keep peace.

Traditional parents and teachers often experienced great difficulty coping with their Creative Children. Some of them felt so disappointed and guilty as parents that they finally gave up. It was only years or decades later when those children became

- 46 -

successful adults and well respected in their fields whether as:

scientists or artists

poets or philosophers

musicians or mystics

actors or athletes

reformers or revolutionaries that their teachers, parents and families appreciated their talent and worth.

Parents and teachers need to be sensitive to the creative needs of all children and especially of those who have Creative Personalities. These children prefer to follow the trails of their hearts rather than the highways of tradition. If their creative efforts are supported, encouraged and appreciated, then those trails become the highways for the next generation. I encourage parents and families to feel proud, rather than embarrassed, of their Creative Children who challenge the traditional norms, and to water the creative plants of their struggles so that one day they can enjoy their creative fruits.

It is not uncommon for Creative Personalities to find themselves in conflict with their traditional educational institutions and misunderstood by their traditional parents and teachers. The experiences of well-respected mystic poet of nineteenth century, Walt Whitman, and the other of a world famous twentieth-century scientist, Albert Einstein highlight this point.

In my book From Islam to Secular Humanism I discussed the Creative and Mystic personalities of poets and mystics and the life story of Walt Whitman:

When we study the life stories of mystic poets we become aware that many of them led simple lives. Because of their aptitude and personalities they did not fit into the formal educational systems and

Dr. K. Sohail

traditional institutions of their times. They were the students of the university of life and learnt from their own experiences. One such example is Walt Whitman, a mystic poet of nineteenth century, who has influenced twentieth-century American literature more than any other poet. Although his poems from his collection Leaves of Grass are taught in colleges and universities all over the world, he himself did not do well in school. His teacher, Mr. Benjamin Halleck, was so disappointed in him that he told his father, "This boy is so idle. I am sure he will never amount to anything."

Whitman's father, agreeing with the teacher, took him out of school at age thirteen and sent him to work in a printer's shop. Even at work he was so preoccupied with his soul-searching that his employer thought he was devoting himself to "the art of doing nothing."

Teacher, employer and father as well as many other people, failed to realize that Walt Whitman was trying to contemplate and meditate upon the mysteries of life from a very early age. (Ref. 1 p. 136)

They could not appreciate the invisible labor that all Creative Personalities have to do before they deliver their masterpieces. Victor Hugo once stated, "A man is not idle because he is absorbed in thought. There is visible labor and there is invisible labor." It is sometimes difficult for artists and writers to explain their creative homework to traditional personalities and families who are not sensitive to the dynamics and workings of the creative imagination. For artists, play is not wasting or killing time. That is when they develop extra-ordinary qualities and create.

Albert Einstein, born in Europe to a Jewish family but was sent to a local Catholic school. Like Walt Whitman, he also did not do well in school and was considered to be a slow learner. His biographer Ronald Clark wrote, "The one feature of his childhood about which there appears no doubt is the lateness with which he learned to speak. Even at the age of nine he was not fluent, while reminiscences of his youth stress hesitancies and the fact that he would reply to questions only after consideration and reflection. His parents feared that he might be subnormal, and it was even suggested that in his infancy he may have suffered from a form of dyslexia." Ronald Clark wonders whether Einstein had been just shy rather than dyslexic as suggested by his son Hans Albert, who says that his father was withdrawn from the world even as a boy - a pupil for whom teachers held out only poor prospects. This is in line with the family legend that when Hermann Einstein asked his son's headmaster what profession his son should adopt, the answer was simply, "It doesn't matter; he'll never make a success of anything." (Ref. 2 p. 10)

After finishing his primary education with difficulty Albert Einstein entered Luitpold Gymnasium, where he spent six years of training and education. That school was quite traditional and did not encourage Einstein's Creative Personality and exploration. Gradually Einstein developed resentment for the school system. His biographer wrote, "The Gymnasium was to leave a critical effect on Einstein in separate ways. The first was that its discipline created in him deep suspicion of authority in general and educational authority in particular. This feeling lasted all his life, without qualification. "The teachers in the elementary school appeared to me like sergeants and in the Gymnasium the teachers were like lieutenant," he recalled. More than forty years later, speaking to the seventy-second Convocation of the State

University of New York, he noted that to him, "the worst thing seems to be for school principally to work with methods of fear, force, and artificial authority. Such treatment destroys the healthy feelings, the integrity, and self-confidence of the pupils." (Ref. 2 p. 13)

But fortunately, in most traditional schools there are a few exceptions. There are teachers who encourage the spontaneity of children and nurture their creativity. They support students to think outside the box and explore their independent thinking and non-traditional lifestyle. Creative students are attracted to such teachers and relatives who support their unconventional passions. Einstein encountered one such teacher. Ronald Clark wrote, "At the Gymnasium there appears to have been, as there is in such schools, one master who stood apart, the odd man out, going his nonconformist way. His name was Reuss. He tried to make his pupils think for themselves while most of his colleagues did little more, in Einstein's later opinion, than encourage an academic kadavergehorsamkeit, "the obedience of the corpse" that was required among troops of the Imperial Prussian army." (Ref. 2 p. 14)

Einstein was also fortunate in his uncle, Casar Koch, who encouraged his independent thinking and nurtured his Creative Personality. Einstein looked forward to his visits and shared his creative and artistic thoughts with him. In his forties he affectionately wrote to his uncle, "You have always been my best-loved uncle....You have always been one of the few who have warmed my heart whenever I thought of you, and when I was young your visit was always a great occasion." Ronald Clark talks about the sharing that took place between Einstein and his favorite uncle. "But some confidence was sparked up between uncle and nephew and it was to Casar that Einstein was to send, as a boy of sixteen, an outline of the imaginative ideas later developed into the Special Theory of Relativity." (Ref. 2 p. 12)

All schools and communities need more teachers like Reuss who encourage independent and nonconformist thinking in their students and uncles like Casar who nurture the Creative Personalities of their nephews and nieces so that we have scientists and artists amongst us. We do not need those principals who discourage parents by stating that their children will "never make a success of anything" and teachers who tell parents with great confidence that their child will "never amount to anything" not knowing that these children and students might be future Einsteins and Whitmans of the world and that their comments might become part of their future biographies.

CHAPTER FIVE

CREATIVE STUDENTS, TRADITIONAL COLLEGES AND UNIVERSITIES

When Creative Students are sent to colleges and universities, they are looking forward to intellectually stimulating environments where they can grow socially and creatively, but they feel disappointed when they find themselves surrounded by traditional books and professors. These students do not find their studies interesting or stimulating and quickly become bored. When they try to be innovative their professors and university authorities do not support them. Some of those students become so disillusioned that they leave, while others get into violent confrontations. Many well-respected scientists, artists, mystics and revolutionaries were perceived as threats by their traditional colleges and universities. The dialogues and debates between those students, their families and academic institutions played a significant role in their choice of professions.

The scientist that comes to my mind in this respect is Charles Darwin. His biographers Michael White and John Gribbin highlight how Darwin's relationship with traditional educational institutions was troubled from the very beginning. Darwin disliked Shrewsbury School where his parents sent him, as it was run by the stern disciplinarian Reverend Samuel Butler.

Charles detested regimented learning and had absolutely no interest in the Classics, which constituted the majority of the curriculum. He regularly cribbed off friends and did the absolute minimum to avoid a beating for laziness or poor test results. As Darwin himself put it, "Nothing could have been worse for the development of my mind than Dr. Butler's school, as it was a strictly classical, nothing else being taught, except a little ancient geography and history. The school as a means of education to me was simply a blank." (Ref. 1 p. 8)

While Charles was languishing in boredom at Shrewsbury, his brother Eras, who was also a Creative Student, was similarly suffering at Cambridge. They used to write and talk to each other to share their frustrations with traditional academic institutions and devise ways to cope with them. White and Gribbin wrote, "Eras hated his work at Cambridge almost as much as his brother continued to detest the Shrewsbury curriculum. Eras found himself taught by dull lecturers and had to endure a seemingly endless succession of calcifying boring discourses. The brothers' correspondence was full of …bitter references to their formal education." (Ref. 1 p. 11)

Such traditional books, teachers and educational environments have negative effects on the minds and personalities of Creative Students. They become disillusioned by their universities and professors and start looking for their own ways to educate themselves and follow their passions and dreams. When Charles' father realized that his son was not benefiting from the classes, he took him out of that school. "In a rare moment of anger Dr. Robert told Charles that he 'cared for nothing but shooting, dogs and rat-catching' and that he would be a disgrace to himself and all his family." (Ref. 1, p. 13)

Charles was sent to medical school to become a doctor like his father, but he did not like medical school as he hated dissection. Luckily he discovered the Plinian Society, whose members engaged in intellectually stimulating discussions, wrote articles about natural history and sciences and critiqued each other's papers. Charles gradually developed an interest in geology, with the result that "during his two years in Edinburgh, [he] learned far more about geology than he did about medicine." (Ref. 1, p.17)

Charles' father was disappointed yet again. This time he took him out of medical school and sent him to a religious school to become a priest. Charles learnt about theology but in his heart he was not convinced about Christian teachings. During his studies in medical school he had become close friends with Robert Grant, a rebel and fellow member of the Plinian Society. The better Charles got to know Robert, the more aware he became of his ideas. Robert was a logical man with a scientific mind who openly criticized Christianity and the Bible as he saw blatant "contradictions between the contents of the Bible and the new findings of science." (Ref. 1, p. 17)

Friendship with Robert Grant and discussions with free thinkers sowed seeds of doubt about God, religion and the Bible that bore fruits when Darwin wrote his books *The Origin of Species* and *The Descent of Man* in which he discussed his disagreements with the traditional teachings of the Bible and Christianity.

It is obvious that Charles Darwin's family, school and university pushed him to follow the traditional path of medicine or theology, while he wanted to follow his heart and become a scientist. The more the father and professors demanded obedience, the harder he rebelled. Finally the family and the university had to give up as they realized that his creativity could not be tamed. Little did his traditional parents realize that they were dealing with a young man whose research and writings would change forever how human beings saw the relationship between Man and God. Little did his Christian teachers foresee that he would try to prove to the world that Man was created in the image not of God, but of an ape. He described and proved human evolution through scientific evidence rather than "by a series of divine interventions." (Ref. 1, p. 17)

Darwin, like many other Creative Students, found the Traditional environments of colleges and universities restrictive and suffocating.

REFERENCE
White, M., and Gribbin, J., *Charles Darwin: A Life in Science*, Toronto: Simon and Schuster, 1995.

CHAPTER SIX

LIVING WITH CREATIVE PERSONALITIES

- THE PRICE OF LOVING KARL MARX

When we study the biographies of creative personalities, whether scientists or artists, poets or philosophers, we become aware that because of their non-traditional lifestyle and their dedication to their creativity, their spouses pay a heavy emotional and social price for loving them. The situation becomes more profound when these personalities become reformers and revolutionaries, as a number of financial, legal and political factors complicate the situation. Spouses must make ongoing sacrifices to maintain a marital relationship.

Karl Marx was no exception. Jenny, his teenage sweetheart, who later became his wife and the mother of his children, suffered in many ways to fulfill the commitment she had made to him in her youth. She had no idea what hardships she would face living with and loving a revolutionary, the creator of *Das Kapital*, and the prophet of Communism.

When we review Jenny's intimate relationship with Karl Marx we become aware of the following struggles.

THE AGONY OF WAITING
After Jenny and Karl Marx fell in love as teenagers,

Creative Minority: Dreams and Dilemmas

Jenny had to wait for seven years before they could get married and live together. Jenny kept her love affair a secret from her family, fearing they would disapprove of Marx who was not of their social status. Additionally, Marx faced educational and financial struggles before he could marry and provide for a family.

During those seven years Marx sent Jenny a number of gifts, love poems and letters sharing his strong feelings for her. He ended one letter, "To my dear, eternally loved Jenny von Westphalen, Berlin, 1836, at the end of autumn". (p. 17) Jenny would respond to his letters with love mixed with anxiety and the fear of an unpredictable future. She wrote, "That I am not in a condition to return your youthful romantic love, I knew from the very beginning and felt deeply even before it was explained to me so coldly, cleverly and rationally. Oh, Karl, my distress lies precisely in the fact that your beautiful, touching passionate love, your indescribably beautiful descriptions of it, the enrapturing images, conjured up by your imagination, that would fill any other girl with ineffable delight, only serve to make me anxious and often uncertain." (p. 21)

FINANCIAL STRUGGLES

Karl Marx, in spite of his pre-occupation with money and finances and efforts to create a philosophy of a political economy for the working class, had no practical sense of managing money. He never had a steady job, a stable income or a secure bank balance. His biographer David McLellan wrote, "With the suppression of the *Rheinsche Zeitung,* Marx found himself once again an unemployed intellectual. His immediate preoccupations were to find a secure job and get married." (p. 59) Even after his marriage his financially uncertain and economically unstable life continued. Such a situation created repeated crises for Jenny who was responsible for paying the bills and looking after the children. Shouldering all the responsibility but with no financial authority, she had to tolerate Marx's financially irresponsible behavior. Often there was no money for food for the children or they had to pawn their clothes and furniture to pay the rent. Such financial hardships created much stress for Jenny who had grown up in a well to do family and had never to worry about day-to-day expenses. On a number of occasions Marx's mother and friends helped him financially.

At one point Marx wrote, "My wife is ill, little Jenny is ill, Lenchen has a sort of nervous fever. I have no money for medicine." He could not even work as a journalist—he had to read newspapers to write his columns and on one typical occasion noted, "I did not write any articles for Dana, because I did not have the penny to go and get newspapers." (p. 242)

THE PAIN OF EXILE AND ARREST

Alongside emotional and financial struggles Jenny had to endure the pain of exile as Marx was unwelcome in his country of residence whether Germany or France because of his political beliefs and journalistic activities, and was forced to move to Brussels or England for his safety. Each time Jenny followed him. McLellan called his life "a long and sleepless night of exile." (p. 231)

Alongside the pain of exile Jenny had to endure the distress of witnessing the arrest of her husband by the police in Brussels. Marx narrated the story in these words: "I was occupied in preparing my departure when a police commissioner accompanied by ten civil guards penetrated into my home, searched the whole house and finally arrested me on the pretext of having no papers...." (p. 178) On one occasion Jenny was picked up and hustled off to the police station. Marx wrote,"...On the pretext of vagabondage my wife was taken to the prison of the Town Hall and locked in a dark room with lost women." (p. 178). The harassment occurred because government authorities believed that through his writings, Karl Marx was inciting people towards revolt and revolution.   McLellan wrote, "…Wilhelm Wolff was arrested and a list of foreigners to be deported was drawn up, with Marx's name at the top."

LIVING WITH A DISORGANIZED MAN
Marx possessed an organized mind but a disorganized and disorderly daily routine, like many creative personalities who do not pay any attention to time or cleanliness. Jenny had to put up with his strange behaviours and routines. A Prussian government spy, describing Marx to a judge, noted that "in private life he is an extremely disorderly cynical human being, and a bad host. He leads a real gypsy existence. Washing, grooming and changing his linen are things he does rarely, and he is often drunk. Though he is often idle for days on end, he will work day and night with tireless endurance when he has a great deal of work to do. He has no fixed times to sleep and wake up. He often stays up all night, and then lies down fully clothed on the sofa at midday and sleeps till evening untroubled by the whole world coming and going through the room."

THE HEARTACHE OF AN AFFAIR
Jenny, who had tolerated many emotional, social and political hardships, was heartbroken when she discovered that Karl Marx had had an affair with a woman far younger than she and had made her pregnant. She wrote in her autobiography, "In the early summer of 1851, an event occurred that I do not wish to relate here in detail, although it greatly contributed to an increase in our worries, both personal and otherwise…"

(p. 249) Marx's biographer McLellan states, "…this event was the birth of Marx's illegitimate son Frederich—the mother was Helene Demuth, 27 years old, and while no beauty, she was nice looking with rather pleasing features. She had no lack of admirers…" To cover up the whole episode and avoid scandal, Karl Marx's friend Frederick Engels, whom Jenny resented because of his womanizing, volunteered to accept legal paternity of the child.

The tragedy was that Jenny could not even discuss the matter with friends and relatives as she was so embarrassed by her husband's behaviour. She was angry, frustrated and depressed but as with many other pains of her intimate life with him, she endured that one in silence.

FEELINGS OF DESPERATION

There were many times in Jenny and Marx's life that they felt depressed and desperate. In 1852 Marx wrote, "When I see the sufferings of my wife and my own powerlessness I could rush into the devil's place…" and later wrote, "I became wild from time to time that there is no end to the muck." Jenny was equally troubled by the chronic state of stress in which they lived. She wrote, "I sit here and almost weep my eyes out and can find no help. My head is disintegrating. For a week I have kept my strength up and I can no more…" (p. 250)

KEEPING THE FLAME OF LOVE ALIVE

In spite of all the hardships Jenny still loved her husband and dedicated her life to him. She was not only his friend and lover but also the mother of his children. Although at times she felt depressed and desperate, she recovered from those episodes and carried on with her life. Marx had not realized how difficult it would be to keep a balance between his political and family lives but he tried his best to be a dedicated father and husband.

His hardships were more political, trying to find a place in the pages of history, while Jenny's hardships were because of her passionate relationship with a revolutionary, trying desperately to find some room in his heart. She knew that he loved her in his bizarre, strange and mysterious way. They exchanged love letters all their lives. In 1856 he wrote in his letter,

"Dear Heart,

Your letter delighted me very much. You need never be embarrassed to tell me everything. If you, poor darling, have to go through the bitter reality, it is no more than reasonable than I should at least share the suffering in spirit? …where can I find another face in which every trait, even every wrinkle brings back the greatest and sweetest memories of my life. Even my infinite sorrows, my irreplaceable losses I can read on your sweet countenance, and I kiss my sorrows away when I kiss your sweet face. "Buried in your arms, awoken by your kisses—that is, in your arms and by your kisses…" (p. 251)

It was letters like this that kept Jenny hoping for better days. In spite of her pains and struggles she loved him dearly till the end of her life.

CHAPTER SEVEN

ANAIS NIN AND THE CREATIVE SELF

When French writer Anais Nin met American novelist Henry Miller in the early part of the twentieth century in Paris, each of them was already married, Anais Nin to a rich businessman, and Henry Miller to June, an actress residing in America. In those days, Henry Miller was a poor struggling artist while Anais Nin was enjoying a financially comfortable existence with her husband. Between Henry Miller and Anais Nin, there evolved a mutual artistic, intellectual and literary seduction. They embarked on a wild and long-standing romance that enriched literature and philosophy, like the relationship of Jean Paul Sartre and Simon de Beauvoir.

During their passionate affair, Nin helped Miller through her financial and emotional support, while Miller encouraged her to continue writing her diaries. Miller predicted that Nin's diary, if published, would be considered one of the masterpieces of twentieth century literature. He was of the opinion that the diary "would take its place beside the revelations of St. Augustine, Petronius, Abelard, Rousseau and Proust". (Ref. 1)

Nin became involved emotionally and sexually not only with her husband and Miller, but also with Miller's wife June, when she came to visit Miller in

Paris. June did not know that her husband had been sleeping with her lover Nin. In addition, Nin was involved with her analyst, Otto Rank, who was a disciple of Freud and who had a great interest in the psychology of writers and the psychopathology of creative people.

Nin's diary chronicled her own struggles and her relationships with her husband, Miller, June and her analyst. She wrote hundreds of pages painting the landscape of her soul. She also wrote a collection of novels, *Cities of the Interior.* Upon her request, Nin's diaries were not published until the 1960s, after the deaths of Miller, June and Nin's husband.

Following the publication of the first volume of her diaries, Nin was invited to lecture all over the world. Nin, who had been a shy girl when she was young, became an eloquent speaker and engaged in passionate and intellectually stimulating discussions with people from all walks of life. She challenged social, moral and political taboos. In the last few years of her life she had two husbands. With one she lived half a year in North America and with the second she spent the other half of the year in Europe. There have been seven volumes of her diaries published so far, as well as a number of collections of her speeches and interviews. Based on Nin's diaries, a feature film, entitled *Henry and June* was made, depicting the lives of the three lovers. Nin has been a source of inspiration for millions of people and a challenge for feminists the world over.

CREATIVE SELF

Nin discovered quite early in life that human beings are socially quite complex and psychologically extremely sophisticated. She saw them as having two sides to their personalities. On one hand there is a

Traditional Self, which is the outcome of conditioning by parents, teachers and cultural norms; and on the other hand a Creative Self, discovered through introspection and soul-searching. Nin had a keen interest in the process by which people discover their Creative Selves. She realized that it was a painful but adventurous process. By discovering their Creative Selves, people are able to be honest with themselves and sincere with others. It is a process of self-liberation, self-discovery and self-actualization.

In her diaries, Nin shares in detail how she went through that journey herself, highlighting the difficulties and the excitements, the frustrations as well as the ecstasies, the blind spots as much as the insights. Nin's diaries are gold mines of knowledge, experience and wisdom, which have touched people over the years and helped them discover their own Creative Selves. She stated that when people get in touch with their Creative Selves, they become very sensitive and "get rid of the defenses which I call the calluses of the soul." (Ref. 1) By discovering their Creative Selves, they also discover their private morality. They transcend religious morality, break the chains of guilt and sin, and enter a world of tranquil hearts and peaceful minds.

An interviewer once remarked to Nin, "Sometimes when you do what you really want to do, you end up hurting people who are very close to you and people you want to remain close to. That can put you in a terrible conflict at times."

Nin answered, "That's the conflict we'll always have. We will always have a conflict between our growth and our fear that that growth will overshadow or injure someone else. And what we have to do is to create our own private morality and our private ethics and our private faith, for that naturally means that if you're a sensitive person you're not going to destroy people around you." (Ref. 2)

CREATIVE THERAPY
Nin believed that if people cannot discover their Creative Self on their own through life experiences, reading books and introspection, then they should seriously consider creative psychotherapy. Such therapy helps people to overcome their inhibitions and insecurities and get in touch with their potential. It helps people to realize that "there is a realm, in which you are all powerful, in which you are the captain of your soul". (Ref. 2) Through this process, people are encouraged to discover their truth and lead healthier, happier and more productive lives. They can then get involved in creative rather than destructive relationships. In therapy there can be a "second birth"…which is a self creation. Nin stated, "…when you go through…the process of self-discovery, you realize that you should not give anybody the power to decide what is right or wrong in your creativity…"(Ref. 2)

CREATIVE RELATIONSHIPS
Nin had experienced a number of unhealthy and painful relationships in her life. Through analysis she developed insights into the negative patterns of intimate relationships. Nin believed that couples act out their unconscious fantasies and the dark sides of their personalities in their relationships. She encouraged people to take responsibility for the roles they play in the evolution of the relationship, rather than blaming everything on the other. She hoped that if people did some soul-searching, they might be able to discover the secrets of honest, sincere and genuine friendships and loving relationships.

Dr. K. Sohail

She believed that in creative relationships, men and women bring out the best in each other and work through the worst parts of their relationships by realizing what they project onto others. She wrote, "Why do I feel entirely responsible for them? I found the answer in Rank, who said that the shadow self, which we don't want to live out, we project onto others. We feel responsible because they are living a part of the self that we are denying; we feel we must protect them from the consequences, for we know that the rebel often pays for his rebellions. In other words, I protected them because I couldn't be as directly a rebel as I am now." (Ref. 2)

CREATIVE EXPRESSION

Nin had developed a great appreciation of the creative process. She believed that creativity expressed itself very differently in women than in men. She was of the opinion that in males, it is more of an intellectual process, but in women the products, like their babies, do not come out of their heads; rather they are born from their wombs. Women nurture their babies as well their creative products with their blood. For them it is a concrete emotional and spiritual experience rather than an abstraction because "woman is closer to the unconscious and remains closer to the unconscious than man, has fewer interferences, and has a less over-developed sense of rationalization." (Ref. 2)

Nin was in touch with the psyche of artists as she was an artist herself; she knew the ecstasies of the writer as she had experienced them herself. She considered writing to be a process of re-creating, of offering a gift of love to others. In one of her interviews she stated, "The white page for me is like a ski slope. I go absolutely mad. I go mad in stationary stores. Just to see beautiful paper gives me a desire to write." When asked in an interview from what source she derived her desire to create, she replied, "From joy! From enjoyment. The way birds sing, I write when I am in love with something - a scene, a character, a book, a country. 'To paint is to love again, Henry used to say'. For me, to write is to love again - to love twice. This is an artist's conviction, that what he is doing is not for himself, it has to be given away." (Ref. 2)

WOMEN'S LIBERATION

Nin believed that for women to liberate themselves, achieving social, economic and legal rights was not enough; they should liberate themselves emotionally and psychologically, gain self-confidence and improve their self-image. She wanted them to improve their self-worth, to like themselves and feel proud of their accomplishments. She wished they could feel special and unique, rather than seeing themselves through the eyes of men. The ultimate goal was for women to liberate themselves from their dependence on men and for men to cease feeling responsible for women. She stated, "I think men will be very much liberated when the women stop trying to live through men vicariously." (Ref. 2) She hoped that with the passage of time, women would overcome their insecurities and inhibitions and leave their inferiority complexes behind. "I want to stress this tremendous lack of confidence, this timidity and fear in woman, because I think that we have talked about the outer obstacles, the legal obstacles, the historical obstacles, the cultural obstacles, even the religious obstacles to her development and her growth. But we haven't focused enough on what happened to woman psychologically." (Ref. 1)

Nin not only liberated herself but also wanted to liberate women of her own and coming generations.

"My dream now doesn't concern just me anymore; it has to do with all women. My dream at the moment is to see women really grow and expand to their full, absolutely fullest capacity." (Ref. 2) She felt connected and committed to the cause, but her approach was quite different than that of other women who were involved in the Feminist Movement. Nin's approach to liberation was more psychological than political, more emotional than social, more creative than anthropological. She was critical of feminists who presented political solutions to women's problems. Nin believed we need to appreciate every woman's problems individually and not lump them all into one social, religious or political abstraction and find one solution for all of them. "We need to be liberated, to think individually. Every woman's problems are different, and they cannot be solved entirely by one formula..." (Ref. 2) Nin thought that women from different cultures needed to find unique solutions for their own unique social environments. She wanted women to discover their own strength and not rely on the social and political changes brought about by men. She believed that once women got in touch with their hidden power, then no man, organization or patriarchal system could exploit, neglect or abuse them. Once they developed self-respect then they could stand on their own two feet and defend themselves in their personal, family and social lives.

Nin was critical of feminists who were angry with men and whose strategy was a feminist revolution that excluded men; she saw women's liberation as intimately connected with that of men. She believed in evolution rather than revolution. When one interviewer opined that women's destructive anger needed to be expressed, and that women needed to "crash through" the historical barriers through revolution, she disagreed. "I think that's a very dangerous track for the women's movement: to think that we can only really become totally grown women, emancipated women, and fulfilled women by breaking off relationships with men." (Ref. 2)

Nin believed that the institutions of marriage and monogamy have played a major role in natural and creative relationships between men and women. She felt that when people try to institutionalize loving relationships they undermine the spontaneity and creativity. For some people marriage might work, but for others it might not. Some people can love only one person intimately, while others can love more than one. There have also been different social expectations of men and women regarding intimate relationships. She believed that we must acknowledge the complexities of intimate relationships and appreciate individual differences. She was aware that experiencing freedom in relationships was a multidimensional phenomenon. When asked if she believed in free love, she replied, "I'm sorry. I can't answer that. It's so individual. I would phrase the answer negatively and say that to me the only crime is not loving. So whatever form of loving you've found, practice it. Whatever form it takes. Because I think the real thing is just to love. Free or not free, married or unmarried, are really things that are too individual. It's different for each individual. There are individuals who are more expansive, there are individuals who are capable of several loves... The idea of multiple relationships has always been granted to men. It will have to be granted to woman." (Ref. 2)

Nin observed than many women after marriage shut the doors of their hearts, minds and souls to other passionate relationships and never reach their full creative potential.

Dr. K. Sohail

CREATIVE COMMUNITIES

Nin was not only involved in women's struggles to liberate themselves, she was also involved in raising people's consciousness generally and making them aware that their personal lives were intimately connected with their social and political lives at a local, national and international level. She believed that a happy man was a blessing but an unhappy man was a curse to society, as his anger, resentment and bitterness were a threat to the social fabric. Gradually such anger and resentment builds up and finally when the leaders of the tribe, based on people's nationality and religion, channel it against another tribe by declaring them enemies, then this cumulative hostility is discharged as acts of war. She stated, "To me war is a multiplication of our own hostilities...." She believed that we are all responsible for wars because we are part of creating an unhappy and unjust environment. She knew that peace was more than absence of war and peace could only last if wedded to justice.

Nin supported an environment where people were not only in touch with their own Creative Selves but also respected other people with different philosophies, who belonged to other tribes from a different ethnic, class, religious and cultural background. She discovered the unity in diversity of people, as she believed that in the depth of our hearts, all human beings are more alike than different, irrespective of the part of the world to which they belong. They might speak different languages but they all share the language of the heart. Nin believed that people could speak the language of the heart when they got in touch with their Creative Selves and changed their consciousness. She stated, "...the great changes in the world will come from a great change in our consciousness." (Ref. 2)

Nin was an extraordinary human being who brought diary writing into the mainstream of literature. She dreamed of a peaceful, loving and compassionate world and a better tomorrow for future generations. Being a writer and a psychotherapist, I have learnt a lot from Anais Nin. I believe she was one of the greatest minds of the twentieth century.

REFERENCES

1. Nin, A., *Diary*, Vol. 1, 1931-1934, Ohio: Swallow
        Press, Ohio University Press, 1975.

2. Nin, A., *"Woman Speaks,"* The Lectures,
        Seminars and Interviews of Anais Nin. Evelyn
        Hinz, E., Ohio: Swallow Press, Ohio
        University Press, 1975.

Dr. K. Sohail

CHAPTER EIGHT

INTERVIEW WITH AN ARTIST NIDA FAZLI

Nida Fazli is one of the most popular writers of India. He is not only a poet but also a screenplay writer for television and films. His *ghazals* (poems) have been composed to music and sung by popular musicians like Jagjeet Singh. In the last few years his autobiography has created a stir in literary circles because of its honesty and literary style. When he was invited to Toronto, I had an opportunity to interview him. I was quite impressed by his philosophy and lifestyle.

Sohail: I feel very excited that I have this opportunity to interview you. You are one of the few writers I know who is popular among intellectuals as well as the general public. You shared with me earlier that in one of your interviews you discussed your philosophy of creativity. Can you share with me your understanding of the creative process?

Nida Fazli: I believe creativity is not a voluntary process. That is why I call it a miracle. If it was a voluntary process then artists could have easily created masterpieces. When we study history we discover that such miracles took place sometimes to some chosen people in some special circumstances. I think the whole process is mysterious. Even great poets like Mirza Ghalib and Meer Taqi Meer are known because of their selected works. That is why I believe that creativity is not a voluntary process.

Once I did an experiment to write poetry voluntarily. I had not written a poem for a while so I picked up a pen and paper and decided to write a poem. Those days I was reading an article that stated that one can learn to create voluntarily. I wrote one line and erased it, I wrote another line and erased it, I wrote a third line and I erased it, as I was not satisfied with them. But then I wrote a line that had the whole poem hidden in it.

I feel every day we get distracted by so many things and people and activities that it becomes very hard for us to concentrate and create. The creative process is like hunting a wild animal in the jungle. Before hunting you have to corner the animal and to do that one needs a lot of time and patience and strategy. Usually I am struck by a line, or an idea or an image and then I pursue it to create a poem. It is the journey from the known to the unknown. It is like the travels of Columbus who did not know where his journey would end. I have to find that line or image that acts as a hook to take out the poem hidden inside me.

When I get up in the morning, I get a little distracted with the movie scripts, a little distracted by the household activities, a little distracted by my idiosyncratic habits, a little distracted by the trees, a little distracted by the beautiful women, a little distracted by the charming children. So it is hard to focus and collect oneself and then create something. A creative relationship is a relationship between a statue and worshipper. He sculpts a statue from a rock and

Dr. K. Sohail

then worships it. By worshipping, the statue gets extraordinary power and then becomes a source of inspiration. A few months ago I met a young woman. I was fascinated by her smile. Later on I fantasized about her, and I felt intoxicated by her smile. That intoxication gave birth to one poem, then a second, then a third. After a while the fantasy lost its spark and I stopped creating poems about her.

Once I did another creative experiment. I go for a walk every morning to the nearby ocean, as I like water. One morning I saw a little five-year-old girl standing at a bus stop. She looked half asleep. She was carrying her school bag. I liked the girl. While I was looking at her, I felt as if the sea and the winds were also looking at her. When I passed close to her, I casually said, "Good Morning." Hearing the greetings from a stranger she became serious. A big seriousness on a small face looked wonderful. For the next few months every morning I said, "Good Morning." I used to imagine how she would look if she smiled. And then one day while I was passing close by, she came running to me and said, "Uncle, I saw you on television last night." And that time she was smiling and looked wonderful. When I asked her about her name, she said, "Shurdha."

Unfortunately the next day the political situation between Pakistan and India got worse and the schools closed in Bombay. I did not see her for a few days. So I went looking for her and met her family and took some pictures of her. Her father was quite fascinated by my interest in his daughter. He asked me, "Why are you taking her pictures? What will you do with them?"

I said, "I will send them to the political leaders of Pakistan and India and tell them that life is more than religious extremism and terrorism. It is Shurdha's wonderful smile too. And then I created a poem called "Shurdha."

I believe the creative process is very complex and mysterious. You will be surprised to know that there is an old tree in front of my house and after breakfast I go and stand under it for a few minutes. If I do not do that, I feel something is missing in my life. I find those moments very inspiring. That tree helps me in completing my poems and developing new ideas.

I find children very inspiring. I enjoy watching them go to school. I carry chocolates and toffees for them in my pocket. All the adults in my neighborhood do not know me but all the children know me very well.

I am also friends with crows. When I moved into my house, a crow used to come to visit me in my studio. During my breakfast I threw a piece of bread for him and he jumped to pick it up. Then he brought some of his friends. They used to come regularly. They were very punctual. If I got late, they used to remind me of my breakfast. They pick up the bread and then go to the tap and drink water that drops from the tap drop by drop. Now I leave some bread for them at night, so that if I sleep in, they get their breakfast. Those crows have helped me develop a sense of responsibility.

In my creative life, my prolonged isolation and loneliness have also played a major role. In 1964-65, my family decided to immigrate from Gavaliar to Karachi, from India to Pakistan. At that time I believed that we could not solve our problems by leaving our homelands. So I decided not to join them and became a stranger in my own home and homeland. I felt lonely for a long time. Because of that loneliness, I developed some attitudes that others might find unethical or anti-social. For example I stopped believing in the institution of marriage. Now the woman I live with is a non-Muslim and because I am a Muslim, our relationship cannot be legalized. For awhile my loneliness had also given birth to fear. I used to lock all the doors and bolt things at night as I used to be scared. I was nervous that someone would come into the house in the middle of the night and kill me. The interesting thing was that during the day, I felt normal.

In short, all I am trying to say is that my relationships with nature, with birds and trees and animals and people, are all connected with my creativity and I find the psychology of creativity quite convoluted but fascinating.

Sohail: Can you share with me some things about your family and your relationship with your parents?
Nida: My father had a colorful personality. He was very popular among women. Before marriage he had a number of liaisons with prostitutes. Even after he was married to my mother, he still used to visit the prostitutes. In my autobiography, I have written about that topic in detail. I have discussed the middle-class values of his time, in which men used to marry one woman to have children and a family but used to be sexually involved with many other women to have fun.

I faced a lot of fear as a child. Dad used to come home late, and my Mom used to get hysterical. All of us were small, so we used to get scared of the evil spirits. My older sister used to put the Holy Quran on the table to protect us from those spirits. We used to wait for our Dad to come home so that we could feel safe and go to sleep. Because of such an environment, all the children reacted strongly.

I cannot say about the psychological reactions

Creative Minority: Dreams and Dilemmas

of my siblings but I became rebellious. My Mom did not want me to socialize with children of lower class but I did not listen to her. I knew it would bother her but I did not care. After getting disillusioned with my Dad, my Mom directed all her affection and love to her children. But it was too much for me. I used to feel the pressure of her love. Her mothering became smothering and I rebelled. I also felt jealous. I thought my Mom preferred my older brother over me. I used to feel neglected, as she would ask me to wear the leftover clothes of my brother. I resented that.

When I look back at the time when my parents moved to Pakistan, I remember that my older brother had moved to Pakistan in 1952. I wonder whether I resented my family joining my brother in Pakistan. Those days Muslim families moved to Pakistan for different reasons. Many Muslims felt they were not treated fairly and justly in India. They believed Pakistan was a paradise for Muslims. Some Muslims were afraid of racial riots while others were worried about their daughters. They thought they could not get suitable Muslim boys for their girls. But I resented my family joining my brother, so I stayed behind. But then I became homeless in my own home. I felt isolated and lonely and alone. After a long time I decided to visit Pakistan to attend a poetry festival and visit my family. Unfortunately everything had changed. My parents had passed away. My relationship with my brothers and sisters had lost all spontaneity and I did not feel at home in their home. So I could stay with them for only a couple of days and then came back.

Sohail: When did you realize that nature had given you a special creative gift and you could become a successful writer and an artist?

Nida: As a child I was not aware of that natural gift but my father had good taste in literature and he used to recite couplets of famous Urdu poets. Because of that literary atmosphere I had developed a taste in poetry. During my student life I used to write poems in the classical tradition of Dagh Dehelvi. Female students used to like my romantic poetry to such an extent that they used those lyrics in their love letters.

And then I faced a tragedy, a romantic tragedy. I started liking a girl in my class. She used to sit at a 45-degree angle in my class and I could only see her back from her short blouse. I was so fascinated by her that even the footpath on which she stepped looked wonderful. I enjoyed looking at her from a distance. Those days I did not have the courage to go and share with her my feelings. And then one day I read a notice on the notice board that she was killed in an accident. She was riding a bike near the temple and got crushed by a truck. After reading that news a wave went through my heart, it was a wave of sadness and depression and confusion. When I looked at the classical Urdu poetry, I could not find a couplet to express my feelings. That day I realized that I have to create my own poetry to share my own unique experiences. I used to wonder why I was so intensely affected by the news, as I hardly knew her. But I felt a special connection with her, even though I never talked to her.

After some time, I was walking close to the temple and I heard someone reciting a religious song in which Radha after separating from Krishna looks at the tree and complains that he just stood still there while she was devastated by the separation from her beloved. That day I realized how I felt connected with the trees. That experience was a turning point in my life. I realized that every pain and every experience had to be expressed in a unique way. At that time I rebelled against the highway of tradition and started walking on the trail of my heart. I left the classical style and started sharing my own observations and experiences and developed my own style in poetry.

Sohail: How old were you then?
Nida: I was in the college doing my B.A. I must have been eighteen or nineteen.

Sohail: Alongside creating poetry you have also been writing prose and screenplays for television and film. What do you think is the difference between serious and popular literature?
Nida: We have inherited many traditions of literature. In that tradition there is a folk tradition and also a religious tradition. We have inherited Kabir's poetry and verses of Quran and mythology of Ramayan. It is amazing to see the broad canvas of Quran. It deals from day to day problems of married life to the dilemmas of war. Great literature used to be for intellectuals as well as for common people. Kabir's poetry is enjoyed by university professors as well as by farmers. It is unfortunate that art and literature have lost touch with the common people and have become the domain of the elite. When that happened fiction writers lost their readership. In Urdu literature writers like Baidi and Ismat Chughtai had more readers than writers like Anwar Sajjad. In Indian tradition Kabir had a great tradition. He used to say, "I write what I see and experience and not what I read as I am an unlettered man." Tagore was influenced by Kabir and because of that folk tradition—he won the Nobel Prize in Literature. But it is unfortunate that critics did not appreciate Kabir in his life. He was ignored for more than two centuries. Many critics

have been misleading the readers.

It is unfortunate that Urdu literature did not evolve a folk tradition and became urbanized too soon. Our Urdu poets are too attached to classical tradition and are nervous to use new words and idioms. Before creating a new expression they read the collections of poetry of Dagh. It is unfortunate that critics are arguing with other critics. Creative people have been ignored and overlooked in serious discussions.

Sohail: As a writer and an artist you have a relationship with both written words and moving images. What do you see as the difference? Some poets and fiction writers do not respect screenplay writers.

Nida: The world of books is very different than the world of films. Both writers move in different worlds. It is not necessary that a good novelist would also be a good screenplay writer. Many successful novels did not become successful films because the story was not successfully transformed to the screen. Paraim Chand's famous novel *The Chess Players* did not become a popular film. One of the issues was historical authenticity. Some characters in history become myths and if they are presented with historical authenticity they lose their appeal, as common people are more interested and fascinated by myths than realities.

The other important factor is the camera. When a written story is presented by the camera, a number of other factors start playing a role. The use of the camera, the distance, the close up, the background, the lighting, the editing, all become important in the film, whereas they are not important in a book. So the grammar of the film story is very different than the grammar of the written novel.

Creative Minority: Dreams and Dilemmas

Sohail: Indian film director Satayajit Ray was ignored during his life. But when he received an Oscar award a few days before his death, he became an overnight celebrity. Why was that, do you think?

Nida: Asians still suffer from colonial hangover. We do not recognize our Eastern writers and artists until they are recognized by the West. The third rate writers of English are more recognized than the first rate writers of our native languages. One such example is Taslima Nasrin. She became famous all over the world by writing an ordinary journalistic novel *Lajja*. As compared to *Lajja*, Bedi's novel *Ik Chadar Maili Si*, Abdullah Hussain's novel *Udaas Naslein* and Qurat-ul-Ain Haider's novel *Aag Ka Darya* are of higher literary value. Taslima's popularity is connected with marketing. The issue is more economic and political than artistic and literary. These days the artist has to fight his war on many fronts. He has to protect his work from the media, as the media tends to pollute the innocence of art and literature. It is hard for writers and artists to remain authentic and candid while dealing with sound bites and advertisements of the media.

Sohail: You are a popular artist and writer and you deal with the media all the time. How has your popularity affected your creativity?

Nida: In one of his interviews Garcia Marquez shared that he has been feeling an inhibition in his creative flow after he received the Nobel Prize. His spontaneity has been affected. I believe an artist and writer takes a long time to develop his image. After developing the image it is even harder to maintain that image. An artist is always growing and when you are growing, you are losing something while you are gaining something. Creative process disconnects you from others and makes you a little alone and lonely. An artist has to keep on reviewing his work and life critically.

Sohail: What do you think of the suffering that artists have to face all their lives?

Nida: I believe that creative people are born three times in their lifetime: the first time from their mother's womb, the second time from society's womb and the third time from their own womb. Some people go to their graves the same way they were born from their mother's womb. They never discover themselves. Discovering oneself and giving birth to oneself is a complex and mysterious process. That is why poets, mystics and prophets spend a lot of time by themselves to get in touch with their inner self, their Creative Self. That is why Mohammad used to go to the cave to spend time with himself, before Quran was revealed to him. That was part of his creative journey and in that journey normal logic does not work as creativity has its own logic. Creative people have to discover their unique lifestyle and logic.

We have no choice of the family, religion, language, community and culture we are born in. But when we study other languages, religions and cultures, they help us in delivering ourselves from our own community. To know thyself is the cornerstone of the creative journey.

An artist tries to transform an abstract into a concrete and presents it to others. To do that he has to work hard and experience life. It requires more than reading books.

Sohail: What are your views about the frustrations artists feel in their life?

Creative Minority: Dreams and Dilemmas

Nida: I believe frustrations are of two types: a negative and a positive. The negative frustration turns into anger, resentment and bitterness, while the positive frustration acts as a source of inspiration and helps the artist to travel from the unknown to the known. An artist is like a child, full of wonder and searching. To a child's eye all views remain fresh and new. They do not get jaded. When Tagore was asked in his old age "Do you have any more to write?" he responded, "In this universe from dust particles to stars there is far more undiscovered than discovered. So we have to keep on learning and growing and creating."

For an artist involvement is important. You cannot be inspired if you are not involved. When I am involved in a woman's smile, it inspires me to create poems. When we are involved with the beauty of words we play with them and create poetry. It is the involvement that creates lullabies and bedtime stories. Many times I am touched by something and I feed my mind's computer with those feelings and thoughts and ideas and wait for the moments of inspiration. And when I am inspired even after days or weeks, I can create the whole poem in a few minutes. As I mentioned earlier I believe the creative process is quite fascinating and mysterious.

Sohail: Thank you for sharing your thoughts today.
Nida: I enjoyed talking to you. I have been reading your poems and stories in Indian magazines. You are creatively very active and that is a great thing.

Note. Special thanks to Rafiq Sultan for transcribing the interview and offering creative suggestions.

Dr. K. Sohail

Creative Minority: Dreams and Dilemmas

CHAPTER NINE

THE SAQI PHENOMENON

You can love him, you can hate him, but you cannot ignore him because he would not let you do that. He will push you and confront you and challenge you and provoke you until you react, until you give him attention. He loves attention. For him, even negative attention is better than no attention. He hates to be ignored. He hates to be dismissed. He loves himself like Narcissus and wants others to love him; and if they don't love him then he hates them and wants them to hate him. Even when they hate him, he feels good, as he is being affirmed and not overlooked or ignored or dismissed. He does not want others to be indifferent towards him. He loves strong reactions, intense emotions. He enjoys drama, rather, melodrama. Everything he does has a dramatic quality to it. He shared with me that people have told him that he should have been an actor rather than a poet. His melodrama gets him into trouble and he loves to be in trouble. He likes to be in the centre of controversy and to achieve that he challenges every literary, social, religious, moral and sexual taboo that he comes across. That is why he is the most controversial personality of the Urdu world. That is why he named his collection of poems *Nailing Dark Storms*. He loves to be in the eye of the storm. To understand the Saqi Phenomenon, on the one hand, we have to understand the evolution of Saqi's personality and on the other hand the dynamics of the social, cultural and religious environment he grew up in. The Saqi Phenomenon is the outcome of the interaction of two extremes - the interaction between an extremely suppressive culture and an extremely rebellious personality, and the interaction between an extremely hypocritical society and an extremely outspoken and cruelly honest character. When two extremes clash there is always a spark and in Saqi's case, he turned it into a flame, into a raging fire and that fire is burning everything and everybody it comes across. Some people feel that the fire might burn Saqi himself more than anybody else. He might be his own worst enemy. It might be like the fire of the alcohol he consumes excessively every day to the point of blackouts, a dangerous proposition. He might transform himself into ashes. N.M.Rushid cremated himself after death while Saqi might cremate himself while still alive. Fire has been a prominent metaphor in his poetry.

> Eik dauzakh tha mere seenay mein
> jis sey chehra mera munawwar tha

Sirf aag peeta hoon jistarah se jeeta hoon
Us tarah se jeene mein uljhanaein bahut see hein

When I ask people their opinion of Saqi, I get a wide range of reactions. On the one extreme is the group that says,

> "Saqi is a genius."

> "He is the most original of all modern Urdu poets."

> "Saqi is carrying the torch lit by Rushid and Meera ji."

> "The history of Urdu poetry will be incomplete without mentioning Saqi's name."

> "We are proud to have known and met Saqi."

On the other extreme is the group that says,

"Saqi is insolent and abusive. He is impudent, contemptuous, impertinent and insulting."

"Saqi is vulgar and obscene."

"He should be ashamed of what he writes."

"There is more drama than poetry in his writings."

"He is the anti-hero of Urdu poetry."

"If Saqi had not written a word, Urdu poetry would not have missed anything."

And then there are others who have realized that he is the only one who can curse and swear at the so-called saints and sadhus and pundits and reformers of art and literature and social morality and expose their hypocrisies and bigotries. He is the only one who can dare to say, "The King is naked."

In spite of Saqi's harsh exterior he has a heart of gold. He is like an orange - bitter peel, sweet pulp. Underneath his provocative and jesting demeanor, he is a loving and caring and kind and affectionate and generous human being. He will give the shirt off his back for his friends. But he can sacrifice his love of friendship for the love of literature. He will not praise a third-rate poem just because his friend wrote it. He is candid and honest in his appreciation of poetry. He will not sacrifice his love of literature for anything in the world except for...his love for his own self. He loves himself more than he loves literature and believes his love for himself is also because he is the best living Urdu poet. But he does not seem fully sure of it so he has to keep on asking and proving and challenging and quoting his friends again and again. He has a superiority complex, which sometimes seems like a reaction to his self-doubts and insecurities. He has not yet reached a stage where he can trust his poetry to speak for itself. He has to blow his own horn

Dr. K. Sohail

not only privately but also publicly. He still has not reached a stage where he can let his admirers like Shams-ur-Rahman Farooqi and Mushfiq Khawaja praise him in their writings; he still needs to keep on quoting them again and again. He is afraid that he might not be remembered. He wants to make sure he has a following like Faiz, Rashid or Mira Ji whom he appreciates and criticizes for different reasons. Some wonder whether he can accept the same honesty and criticism from others as he dishes out to the whole world. Saqi says, "Yes." Others have their doubts.

All the lovers of Urdu poetry are convinced that Saqi is a great poet and will be remembered in Urdu literature for a long time. The only one who does not seem fully convinced is Saqi himself. After spending a day with Saqi and interviewing him for a couple of hours, I remained under Saqi's spell for a few days. I realized that Saqi has more depth to his character than appears on the surface. It seems ironic that he is himself a distraction from people getting in touch with his deeper self. His overwhelming personality and constant talk make it very difficult for others to have a meaningful dialogue with him. I was lucky to obtain a detailed interview with him, which helped me understand some aspects of his personality and poetry. I wonder whether he ever lets his dear ones share their silences with them.

Saqi's love for animals had always been a mystery. It was helpful to learn that his father who was a veterinary surgeon provided an atmosphere for Saqi to mingle with cats and dogs in his formative years. Those experiences left lasting impressions on Saqi's personality. There is also an element of guilt. Saqi's accompanying his servant to the pond to drown tomcats in bags was a significant event in his childhood. Saqi identifies with the animals, with the

Creative Minority: Dreams and Dilemmas

underdogs, with the victims. One can see a relationship with Kafka's story Metamorphosis...a metaphor of modern literature and life.

Saqi was quite honest, open and candid about his sexual experiences, which is very rare these days. Most writers and artists from the East are very secretive. They remember the fate of Josh Malihabadi who got into deep trouble after publishing his biography *Yadon Ki Barat* and being open about his homosexual encounters. Saqi did not hesitate to talk about his promiscuous life in England, sharing the story of a sexually starved man from a sexually inhibited Eastern society overindulging in the sexually open atmosphere of the Western world. I was surprised that the phase lasted for only three years. I was further surprised to learn that Saqi has been faithful to his wife and monogamous for thirty years. I think his marriage provided an anchor to his restless soul; otherwise I would not have been surprised if he had had a nervous breakdown like his mother. After Saqi's interview I would have liked to interview his wife in detail to find out how she coped with him for thirty years. Most people have a hard time coping with him for thirty hours. I have a lot of respect for her even without meeting her.

Even the anchor of his marriage, a stable job and permanent residence could not save him completely and he became an alcoholic. He told me that his daughter, who is an addiction counselor, suggested that he see a therapist but he turned her offer down. Maybe like Virginia Wolf he believes that the therapist is "the rapist of the mind" and like Edvard Munch worries that by getting rid of his eccentricities and idiosyncrasies and insanities, he might also lose his creativity.

Saqi was also open in sharing how he was spoiled

and pampered as a child. He himself wished that he had been disciplined at a young age, which might have brought some balance into his life. Saqi's rebellious personality is a mixed blessing. On the one hand, it gives him courage to challenge every tradition and taboo and cliché, but on the other hand pushes those people away who might have learnt a lot from him and from whom he would have learnt a lot. People are nervous about coming close to him because they aren't sure when he will blow the whistle. I myself had been nervous for a long time about meeting him and interviewing him. I was encouraged when he wrote me an affectionate letter praising one of my short stories. I am even nervous sending him this interview and essay, unsure of his reactions.

I do admire his honesty and openness, which is becoming a rarity in a hypocritical society, but I am also aware that his honesty can be cruel too. Saqi is unpredictable but we can be sure of one thing. People might find his company exciting or traumatic but they will never find him boring. I have no doubt that Saqi will be remembered for a long time. I am not sure though whether he will be famous or infamous. He belongs to the club of the Oscar Wildes and S. H. Muntoes of the world. I feel fortunate to have spent some time with him. He is not a character one can ever forget.

Part Two

Creativity and Insanity

CHAPTER TEN

CREATIVITY AND INSANITY

A poet is an unhappy being whose heart is
torn by secret suffering, but whose lips are
so strangely formed that when the sighs
and cries escape, they sound like beautiful
music.

Soren Kierkegaard

The idea that creativity and insanity are interrelated is
not new, although it has been transformed over the
centuries depending upon our understanding of both
processes and their dynamics. The ancient Greeks had
a concept of "divine madness" wherein madness
meant not only mental illness but also a state of mind
in which human beings were possessed with spirits
and inspired by gods. Certain gods offered different
kinds of inspiration: Apollo for knowledge of the
future, Eros for love and the Muses for song and
poetry. They also had a word for that process,
enthusiasm, meaning "god within." (Ref. 2)

Socrates declared, "If a man comes to the door of
poetry untouched by the madness of the Muses,
believing that technique alone will make him a good
poet, he and his sane compositions never reach
perfection, but are utterly eclipsed by the
performances of the inspired madman." Aristotle
asked, "Why is it that all men who are outstanding in

Creative Minority: Dreams and Dilemmas

philosophy, poetry or the arts are melancholic?"

The notion that creativity and insanity are interconnected has been reflected in the writings of many writers, artists and philosophers over the centuries. Robert Burton in the seventeenth century noted, "All poets are mad." (Ref. 3)

Some artists observed that insanity ran in families. Van Gogh in one of his letters wrote, "The root of the evil lies in the constitution itself, in the fatal weakening of families from generation to generation...the root of the evil certainly lies there, and there is no cure for it." (Ref. 4)

In the nineteenth century psychologists and psychiatrists began to study the families of artists and psychotics more seriously. Italian psychiatrist Cesare Lombrosa was the first scientist to make an association of mental illness with creativity, but he was overenthusiastic in his conclusions. He believed that all creative people were mentally ill. He gave examples of Schopenhauer, Beethoven, Dostoevsky and many others to prove his hypothesis. (Ref. 5) But it was only in the twentieth century that the research methodology became sophisticated enough and the studies of families of psychotic and creative people extensive enough to provide reliable results. In the second half of the twentieth century, scientists proved that not only did insanity and creativity run in families but that the two could also be found in the same families.

Family studies of people suffering from schizophrenia and manic-depressive illnesses (which affect about one per cent of the population) show that both illnesses are far more present in the first-degree relatives of patients. A number of studies clearly show that both forms of mental illness are genetically transmitted and family members of those mentally ill people are more at risk to suffer from mental illness than the general population.

Other family studies in Europe and North America have shown that creative people and their relatives are more at risk to suffer from mental illness than the general population and that creativity and insanity are genetically transmitted in the same families. It is also important to note that the expression of creativity is generalized and not specific to the form. Creative people could be writers, artists, musicians or dancers. (Ref. 6)

What is common to creative people and psychotics? It is generally accepted that both groups perform outside the range of normal behaviour with their non-traditional thinking and unconventional lifestyles, both deal with the unconscious mind and both transform the world around them. The difference in them according to American psychiatrist Silvano Arieti is, "Both the creative person and the psychotic want to transform the world but…their transformations are quite different. The creative person wants to change reality to beautify it or enlarge the field of human knowledge or experience in order to provide usefulness, understanding and predictability or to evoke a universal response. The psychotic instead wants to transform reality in a way that fits his private ways of feeding his delusional thinking and does so in ways which do not evoke consensus but often remain strictly individualistic, bizarre, strange, incommunicable and even destructive to self and others." (Ref. 7)

One of the important questions mental health professionals face is how to deal with a creative person who has a psychotic episode and suffers from schizophrenia, depression or some other form of mental illness. Artists also wonder about the relationship between the periods of creative expression and psychotic regression.

Some creative people when faced with emotional suffering and mental illness are quite willing to receive treatment, whether medications or psychotherapy or a combination of both, to control their symptoms; but others feel that the medications will interfere with their creativity. They believe that creativity and insanity are part of a package deal. Rather than having none of them they prefer to have both.

Edvard Munch, who had been hospitalized on a number of occasions for his depressive episodes, said, "A German once said to me, `but you could rid yourself of many of your troubles.' To which I replied, 'They are part of me and my art. They are indistinguishable from me and it would destroy my art. I want to keep my sufferings.'" (Ref. 1)

In the last few decades there has been a wide range of medications discovered that control many symptoms of mental illness. The medications range from antipsychotics to antidepressants to Lithium Carbonate which has been found quite effective in controlling the symptoms of manic depressive illness.

In 1979 Drs. Polatin and Fieve wrote, "In the creative individual who does his best work in the course of a hypomanic period the complaint regarding the continued use of Lithium Carbonate is that it acts like a `brake.' These patients report that Lithium Carbonate inhibits creativity so that the individual is unable to express himself, drive is diminished, and there is no incentive. These patients also indicate that when they are depressed, the symptoms are so demoralizing and so uncomfortable they welcome the `mild high' when depression disappears and prefer to settle for a cyclothymic's life of highs and lows rather than an empathic middle of the road mood state achieved through the use of Lithium Carbonate." (Ref. 4)

But when such a concern was put to the test and creative people were assessed regarding their creative expression following treatment with Lithium Carbonate, most of them agreed that their creativity had actually increased. They admitted that the control of symptoms with medications had actually improved their concentration. Only a small number stopped medications because of adverse side effects.

There are also mixed feelings expressed by writers as well as therapists on the role of psychotherapy in dealing with artists' unresolved conflicts. On one extreme are the writers like Virginia Woolf who considered psychotherapy as "the rape of the mind" (Ref. 8) and on the other there are therapists who feel that artists can enrich their personal and creative lives through therapy. Myron Marshall wrote, "Some creative artists seek psychotherapy because they wish to overcome inhibitions that interfere with the free exercise of their talents." (Ref. 9)

Some therapists see psychotherapy in itself as a creative process that enhances growth in the patient as well as the therapist. Albert Rothenburg in his article *Creativity and Psychotherapy* writes,

> ...both patients and therapists are oriented to and engaged in, facilitating creation. Both are focused on the patient's creation of aspects of his or her personality, and both are engaged in an ongoing mutual creative process that involves the patient's personality, attributes and structure.

Creative Minority: Dreams and Dilemmas

By creation of personality attributes and structure I mean something directly analogous to creative in the prototypical areas of arts and sciences. In the latter areas, creation and creativity are most meaningfully defined as the production of something both new and valuable (Rothenburg and Hausman, 1976). In psychotherapy there also is the production of both the new and the valuable. The patient develops better personality attributes and structure. These are valuable both to the patient and society at large. (Ref. 10)

Many experts believe that the future of humanity depends upon the insights of creative people, whether scientists, artists, mystics or social reformers, who guide us to the next step of human evolution. Even when they suffer, they suffer on behalf of all of us, so we must cherish and celebrate their achievements. Kay Jamison wrote, "The great imaginative artists have always sailed `in the wind's eye' and brought back with them the words or sounds or images to `counter balance human woes.' That they themselves were subject to more than their fair share of these woes deserves our appreciation, understanding and careful thought." (Ref. 4)

Art is a form of therapy. Sometimes I wonder how all those who do not write, compose or paint can escape the madness, the melancholia, the panic-fear inherent in the human situation.

Graham Green

Dr. K. Sohail

REFERENCES

1. Panter, B., *Creativity and Madness*, USA:
    Aimed Press, 1995.

2. Ludwig, A., MD. *"Reflections On Creativity and
    Madness"*, American Journal of Psychotherapy,
    USA, January 1989.

3. Burton, R., *Anatomy of Melancholia*, Floyd Dell and
    Pane, Jordan Smith, E., New York: Tudor,
1948.

4. Jamison, K., *Touched With Fire - Manic Depressive
    Illness and the Artistic Temperament*, Canada:
    The Free Press, 1994.

5. Arieti, S., *"From Primary Process To
    Creativity"*, Journal of Creative Behaviour, Vol.
    12, No. 4.

6. Anderson, Nancy, MD, Ph.D. "Creativity and
    Mental Illness: Prevalence Rates in Writers
    and Their First Degree Relatives", American
    Journal of Psychiatry, USA, Oct. 1987.

7. Arieti, S., Creativity - The Magic Synthesis, Basic
    Books Inc. Publisher, New York, 1976.

8. Monore, R., Creative Brainstorms, Irvington
    Publishers Inc., New York, USA, 1992.

9. Marshall, M., "Lithium,Creativity and Manic
    Depressive Illness", Academy of
    Psychosomatic Medicine, Oct. 1970.
10. Rothenberg, A., "Creativity and Psychotherapy",

Psychoanalysis and Contemporary Thought, Vol. 7 #2, 1984.

Creative Minority: Dreams and Dilemmas

CHAPTER ELEVEN

VIRGINIA WOOLF: A WRITER WITH "VIOLENT MOODS OF THE SOUL"

Virginia Woolf was fortunate and unfortunate at the same time. While she touched the heights of creative expression and wrote novels that, even more than fifty years after her death are still held in high esteem, she also suffered from repeated episodes of depression and finally took her own life by filling her coat pockets with rocks and walking into the water to drown herself. Throughout her life, creativity and insanity seemed to be intimately connected. Most of her depressive episodes took place "after the novels had been submitted for publication but while she was awaiting critical reviews." (Ref. 2)

A study Woolf's life shows a number of very intriguing associations. Her family seemed to be blessed and cursed at the same time - blessed with a number of artists and writers and cursed with a number of people who suffered from manic - depressive illness, some of whom needed to be hospitalized and treated. Her family provides proof to research workers who believe that creativity and insanity are not only hereditary but also run in the same families. Children of those families are born with

- 103 -

a predisposition to non-traditional thinking and
lifestyles. Those who are strong and can face the
dilemmas become artists, those who are weak and
vulnerable have nervous breakdowns, while there are
others who experience both extremes, and Virginia
Woolf was one of them. (Ref. 1)

Thomas Caramango documented in impressive
detail the generations of depressive and
manic-depressive illness in Virginia Woolf's family.
(Ref. 1) Kay Jamison writes, "Her grandfather, mother,
sister, brother, and niece all suffered from recurrent
depressions, her father and another brother were
cyclothymic, and her cousin James, who had been
institutionalized for mania and depression, died of
acute mania." (Ref. 1) Alma Bond noted, "Virginia's
great-grandfather, grandfather, uncle and cousin were
all prominent authors. Her mother was Julia Jackson,
herself a published writer and the granddaughter of a
French nobleman who was page to Marie Antoinette.
Virginia's sister, Vanessa, became a celebrated painter
who married the critic Clive Bell, while her brother,
Adrian, was a distinguished psychoanalyst, writer and
editor." (Ref. 3)

Virginia Woolf's mother, who also suffered from
depression, could not provide the nurturing and
caring that the young Virginia needed for her
emotional growth and maturity. She once wrote,
reminiscing about her mother, "I can see now that she
was living on such an extended surface that she had
not time, nor strength, to concentrate upon me. Can I
ever remember being alone with her for more than a
few minutes?" (Ref. 4)

Alma Bond feels Woolf's mother "appeared to be a
narcissistic woman, who required constant
affirmation, and thus was unable to respond to the
needs of a developing child." (Ref. 3) Woolf was an

Creative Minority: Dreams and Dilemmas

emotionally deprived child, which undermined her self-esteem and self confidence. "Virginia showed traits of an episodic disorder as a young girl. It was said that she had sudden extremes of emotion which would range from rage, to gloom, to ecstasy. It was also noted that Woolf herself realized that she had a problem with her sense of 'self' as she reports having memories without a 'self.'" (Ref. 3)

Woolf's parents had children from previous marriages, and she and her sister Vanessa were both sexually abused by their half-brothers. (Ref. 2) That experience undermined Woolf's normal sexual development.

Woolf, in spite of her difficulties, was quite attached to her mother and when she died she experienced her first nervous breakdown at the age of thirteen. She experienced her second depressive episode when her father died when she was twenty-two. (Ref. 2)

Woolf experienced a number of difficulties in her intimate life. She had some lesbian experiences before she married Leonard. Because of the history of mental illness Woolf and her husband decided not to have children and over the years they became more friends than lovers, their marriage sexless. Leonard was a very caring husband who nursed Woolf for months whenever she had depressive episodes. In 1922 while still married to Leonard, Woolf became attracted to the bluestocking writer Vita Sackville-West. They became good friends and then lovers, a relationship that was to be the most significant and long-lasting in each of their lives. Woolf called it a "soul-friendship." They inspired each other for a number of years during which they produced the best of their creative works. Vita had some insights into Woolf's personality and art that Leonard lacked. "Vita realized that her friend's art required her to be in society, something that Leonard did not understand. She realized that Woolf based her fiction primarily upon observations, not upon imagination." (Ref. 5) Over the years Vita lost sexual interest in Woolf and they remained friends for a while but when Vita became intimately involved with Gwen St. Aubyn, whom Woolf disliked, the relationship between Vita and Virginia Woolf ended. Woolf wrote, "My friendship with Vita is over. Not with quarrel, not with a bang, but as ripe fruit falls...." (Ref. 5)

Albert Rothenberg believes that conflict enhances creativity and that homosexuality in writers and artists is a mixed blessing; it makes their life more difficult but also more creative. "Conflict is a prime requisite for the motive to create artistically, and homosexuality is only one of many conflict - ridden conditions responsible." (Ref. 6)

Virginia Woolf as a young writer was full of fears, insecurities and self-doubt. She was afraid she would fail as a writer. She wrote in her diary, "What I had feared was that I was dismissed as negligible." (Ref. 4) She would ask herself, "Is the time coming when I can endure to read my own writing in print without blushing-shivering and wishing to take cover?" (Ref. 7) She worried what others would think about her writings: "...when I write a review I write every sentence as if it were going to be tried before three Chief Justices." (Ref. 4)

By the age of forty she had become quite confident as a writer. She wrote in her diary, "There is no doubt in my mind that I have found out how to begin (at forty) to say something in my own voice; and that interests me so that I feel I can go ahead without praise." (Ref. 4)

"I am to write what I like; and they are to say what they like. My only interest as a writer lies, I begin to see, in some queer individuality; not in strength, or passion, or anything startling, but then I say to myself, is not 'some queer individuality' precisely the quality I respect?" (Ref. 7) "The truth is that writing is the profound pleasure and being read the superficial." (Ref. 4)

She reached a stage where she could write, "I can write and write and write now: the happiest feeling in the world." (Ref. 4) She gradually emerged as a very confident writer and was a source of inspiration for many women.

Virginia Woolf had a keen interest in women's dilemmas and struggles. Her book *A Room of One's Own* and lectures about women's fiction and professions are milestones in feminist literature. She believed that "a woman must have money and a room of her own if she is to write fiction." (Ref. 8) She was aware that although financial freedom was intimately connected with intellectual and artistic freedom, the prevailing social, legal and political restrictions made it impossible for women to be financially independent. She felt that men had to be educated to support, encourage and cherish women's achievements and accomplishments because, "The future of fiction depends very much upon what extent men can be educated to stand free speech in women." (Ref. 9)

She encouraged women to develop independent thinking and hold their own views about life because she felt that in creative writing, "...you cannot even review a novel without having a mind of your own, without expressing what you think to be the truth about human relations, morality and sex." (Ref. 9)

Woolf cautioned women writers that if they wanted to produce great fiction and masterpieces in literature then they had to go beyond anger, resentment and bitterness because "women's writing has suffered in the past from the intrusion of feminist anger." (Ref. 9) She believed that a genuine artist and writer is in touch with the essence, the soul, the spirit of humanity, which transcends sexual and gender bias. Of great writers in the history of mankind she wrote, "They are not men when they write, nor are they women. They appeal to the large tract of the soul which is sexless; they excite no passions; they exalt, improve, instruct, and man and woman can profit equally by their pages, without indulging in the folly of affection or the fury of partisanship." (Ref. 9)

Woolf made such a mark on literature and her times that British Weekly once called her "the ablest of living women novelists." (Ref. 4) T.S. Eliot claimed that she was "the centre of the literary life of London." (Ref. 9)

It is unfortunate that although Wolfe, in collaboration with Leonard, published a number of books on human psychology and psychoanalysis in their Hogarth Press, she did not receive therapy herself. She called therapy "the rape of the mind." "Both believed that madness contributed to Virginia's creativity and that it would be better for Virginia to be periodically psychotic than being 'analysed and ordinary.'" (Ref. 2) Leonard looked after her till her last days.

When Woolf finally decided to commit suicide in March 1941 at the age of 59, she wrote an affectionate letter to Leonard acknowledging his love and care for her. She said, "Dearest, I feel certain I am going mad again. I feel we can't go through another of those terrible times. And I shan't recover this time. I have begun to hear voices, and I can't concentrate. So I am doing what seems the best thing to do. You have given me the greatest possible happiness. You have been in every way all that anyone could be. I don't think two people could have been happier till this terrible disease came. I can't fight any longer." (Ref. 4)

It is interesting to see how Woolf used her psychotic experiences in her fiction. She utilized even her sufferings to enrich her art and her life. She wrote, "As an experience, madness is terrific I can assure you, and not to be sniffed at; and in its lava I still find most of the things I write about. It shoots out of one everything shaped, final not in mere driblets, as sanity does. And the six months — not three — that I lay in bed taught me a good deal about what is called oneself." (Ref. 4) She also believed that literature should be read "with a view to answering certain questions about ourselves." (Ref. 4)

Virginia Woolf has remained a highly regarded name in literature and a mystery to writers as well as psychologists over the decades.

REFERENCES:

1. Jamison, K., *Touched With Fire* - Manic Depressive
   Illness and the Artistic Temperament, The Free Press Canada, 1994.

2. Monroe, R., Creative Brainstorms, Irvington, Publishers Inc., New York, USA, 1992.

3. Panter, B., *Creativity and Madness*, Aimed Press, USA,
   1995.

4. Woolf, V., A Writer's Diary, E. Leonard Woolf, Triad Grafton Books, London, England, 1978.

5. Chadwick, W., and de Courtivron, I.,
   Significant Others, Thames and Hudson Ltd., London, 1993.

6. Rothenberg, A., *Creativity and Madness*, The John Hopkins University Press, Baltimore, Maryland, USA, 1990.

7. Bell, Q., Virginia W., - A Biography, Harcourt Brace and Company, Florida, USA, 1974.

8. Woolf, V., *A Room of One's Own*, Flamingo, Harper Collins Publishers, Glasgow, 1976.

9. Woolf, V., *Women and Writing*, edited by Michele Barrett, Quadrant Editions, Canada, 1984.

CHAPTER TWELVE

VINCENT VAN GOGH
~ AN INSANE GENIUS

Vincent Van Gogh gave a new meaning to colours. He discovered a new language to express human feelings, thoughts, conflicts and dreams. He raised new questions about the relationship between creativity and insanity. His life and his work have remained an enigma for artists as well as mental health professionals. Psychiatric textbooks commemorate his self-amputation of an ear with the diagnosis of Van Gogh's Syndrome, a diagnosis given to mentally ill people who amputate a body part in a fit of psychosis.

When we review Van Gogh's life we find it full of tragic and creative incidents, circumstances and happenings. Van Gogh was born in Holland on March 30th, 1853. His father Theodorus was a minister with a great interest in religious studies, while his mother Anna was a housewife with artistic talents. A year before van Gogh's birth an older brother, also named Vincent, died. One wonders about the impact on Van Gogh of visiting his brother's grave and seeing a tombstone with his own name.

Even as a child, the shy and introverted Van Gogh felt closer to nature than to other human beings. He would spend hours watching birds and animals. He was quick to anger, as small things irritated him. Growing up, nobody saw him smiling or laughing.

Dr. K. Sohail

Van Gogh was always ambivalent about his father, loving and hating him at the same time. His father considered him a strange boy and his mother thought that he always took the longest and hardest route in life.

Van Gogh never liked formal education. When he was sent to a boarding school he left his studies halfway through, worried that formal training and education might suffocate his creativity. He had a passion for his art from an early age, and when he was sixteen he found a job with an art dealer who supplied paintings to art centres in Europe.

Van Gogh worked with that art dealer for five years. When his brother Theo started working in the same store they became good friends and for the rest of his life he wrote hundreds of letters to Theo.

In 1874 when Van Gogh was transferred to London to work, he faced a number of crises. The first was an unsuccessful love affair. Van Gogh fell in love with Ursula, his landlady's daughter. He was too shy to express his feelings and finally when he found enough courage to tell her that he loved her he was devastated to learn that she was already engaged. He requested her to break her engagement but she turned his offer down. Van Gogh was so broken-hearted that he lost interest in his art for a time and resigned from his job.

After withdrawing from art and love, he joined a school to teach. He even studied and preached religion for a while like his father but those distractions did not last long. During that time, Van Gogh was quite emotionally disturbed, and a tragic incident 1877 at the school where he was teaching changed the course of his life. A mischievous student tugged on his coat from the back to tease him. Van Gogh felt so angry and humiliated that he hit the child. That was the first time Van Gogh had lost control in public, but he was dismissed from his job.

In 1880 when Van Gogh recovered from his existential crisis he realized that the only way for him to survive was to dedicate his life to his art and not worry about what others thought of him as a person or as an artist. After that realization Van Gogh embraced his art wholeheartedly. In 1880 he moved to Brussels to learn to sketch and paint and spend time with the established artists.

In 1881 Van Gogh faced another romantic crisis. He fell in love with his cousin Kee, a widow with a child. When expressed his love to her, she could not reciprocate as she was still grieving the death of her husband. He was broken-hearted once again. He was so upset by that crisis that on one occasion in the presence of Kee's parents he held his hand in the flame of a candle long enough that everybody in the room could smell the burning flesh. That was the first time Van Gogh had hurt and tortured himself publicly.

Van Gogh moved from Brussels to The Hague, where he fell in love with a pregnant prostitute. He lived with her for a year and a half and was very affectionate to her son.

When Van Gogh got tired of living in The Hague, he moved to the city of Arles in southern France where he met the artist Adolph Monticelli for whom he had a lot of admiration. Van Gogh's artistic life formally started with his sketches in 1881. In 1883 he started to paint and over the next seven years of his life he created nearly 800 paintings.

Van Gogh's admission to hospital was precipitated by his cutting off his ear on December 24th, 1888. During that psychotic episode he heard voices telling him "Kill him, Kill him." Some people think that during his religious period he had read in the Bible "If thine ear offend thee cast it forth", which he acted upon when he became ill.

During the next eighteen months Van Gogh experienced eight psychotic episodes ranging from a few weeks to a few months but he continued to paint in spite of his illness. He created 450 paintings during those eighteen months. During that time he wrote to his brother almost every day. He described his psychotic episodes as "spells", "fits" and "inner seizures of despair." He even wondered whether his mental illness was constitutional and hereditary. He wrote to his brother, "The root of the evil lies in the constitution itself, in the fatal weakening of families from generation to generation...the root of the evil certainly lies there, and there is no cure for it."

When we focus on the clinical condition of Van Gogh we find a number of opinions. There is no doubt that Van Gogh had a schizoid personality and suffered from psychotic episodes but there is no agreement on the nature of psychosis. Some clinicians feel he suffered from schizophrenia while others believe he was affected by manic-depressive illness. Some mental health professionals think he had epilepsy while others are convinced that Van Gogh like his role model Morticelli was under the influence of hallucinogenic drugs. Morticelli was known to use Absinthe while Van Gogh abused L.S.D. Psilocybin, Mescaline and Absinthe.

After eighteen months of suffering and anguish Van Gogh shot himself in the stomach on July 27th, 1890. He was found dying in terrible pain outside his room. His brother Theo was summoned right away, and Van Gogh died in his arms two days later.

There have been a number of theories about Van Gogh's suicide. Some people believe that he was so dependent on his brother that when he found out that

Theo was sick he could not imagine living without him. He had told Theo in one of his letters that if he died, he would be so devastated, he would commit suicide. Others believe that when Van Gogh realized that not only were people starting to appreciate his paintings, but also that someone had bought one, he decided to end his life — he was too frightened to face his success. He had once written to his mother that the most dangerous thing for a painter is his success and fame.

Van Gogh's mental illness became an inspiration through which his pain was transformed into hundreds of paintings that changed the history of art. Van Gogh might have been insane but there was no doubt that he was a genius who enriched humanity with his creative gifts. His insanity was a catalyst for his creativity.

REFERENCES

1. Stone, I., *Lust for Life*, Penguin Books, New York, 1984.

2. Denvir, B., Van Gogh, Octopus Books Ltd., London, 1981.

3. Van G., Vincent, The Letters of Vincent Van Gogh, Mark Ruskell, Editor, Fontana Paperbacks, London, 1985.

Part Three

Creativity and Psychotherapy

Creative Minority: Dreams and Dilemmas

CHAPTER THIRTEEN

CREATIVE PERSONALITIES ~ THREE GROUPS

I divide the Creative Personalities I have met socially and professionally into three groups.

The first group consists of Creative Personalities who are happy, healthy and successful. They have found a balance between their Creative and Traditional Selves and harmony with their environments. They have resolved their conflicts with their traditional relatives, colleagues and neighbors and have developed a supportive social network that helps them in their day-to-day lives as well as in crises. Such Creative Personalities do not need to see a psychotherapist.

The second group includes Creative Personalities who have minor emotional and social problems. They have unresolved conflicts with their Traditional Selves, family and community. They go through minor crises in their lives but do not require professional help as they learn to accept such issues as part of their character and lifestyle. They do not experience emotional and social breakdowns.

The third group is comprised of Creative Personalities who have serious emotional, family and social problems that cause emotional pain for them and their dear ones. They experience unresolved conflicts between their Traditional and Creative Selves that require professional help. Such people suffer from family conflicts and bouts of anxiety and depression, and may have psychotic episodes. It is unfortunate that most traditional mental health professionals are not educated and trained to deal with Creative Personalities. Such traditional doctors, nurses and therapists treat the anxiety, depression and paranoia but ignore the creative aspect of the personality. Such a situation is most frustrating for Creative Personalities, as they feel misunderstood by the therapists and furthermore they fear that medications and therapy will interfere with their creativity.

I feel that it is our responsibility as mental health professionals to find better ways to deal with the unique issues of this Creative Minority. We need to focus not only on clinical issues but also on their unique personalities. Being a creative person and therapist myself, I have discovered that getting in touch with our patients' creativity and finding healthy ways to express their dark side of personality plays a significant role in their healing and recovery. Over the years as I became more aware of the special needs of Creative Personalities, I was able to better help them. In this section I will share some my therapeutic encounters with Creative Personalities who had serious emotional, educational, professional and social problems and were significantly benefited by a combination of individual, family and group therapy. Medications were prescribed as a last resort if psychotic symptoms were interfering with creative psychotherapy. I hope mental health professionals find this section helpful in developing a special sensitivity to the special needs of Creative Personalities.

CHAPTER FOURTEEN

CREATIVE TEENAGERS AND PSYCHOTHERAPY

I have worked with a number of creative teenagers who were suffering because they were in conflict with their families and schools. Some of them were anxious and depressed, while others were angry. Some had left schools voluntarily while others had been kicked out. Few had any steady income so they were financially dependent upon their parents. Some of these parents had been supportive for a while but were gradually losing their patience. In some families one parent was sympathetic and the other was frustrated, which had created tension in the family. Many parents believed that their teenagers were lazy and were using their creativity as an excuse to cover up their irresponsibility.

Many teenagers that I worked with had a strange schedule. They were up all night reading, writing, painting, drawing or listening to music or talking to their creative friends all over the world on MSN or surfing the Internet and then sleeping all day long. I used to give them late afternoon appointments as they frequently slept in and missed morning appointments, which created big fights in the family. These teenagers did not take care of their clothes or food or health. They believed they were carefree while their parents perceived them as careless, wasting their lives away. Their families called some of those teenagers "bums" and "losers" and "parasites", which they found rude, offensive and insulting.

It was interesting for me to note that these parents believed that their children had serious emotional and mental problems and were in need of "psychiatric" or "professional" help, while these teenagers felt strongly that they were not "crazy" and did not need to see a "shrink."

Before I met these teenagers, some of them had seen a number of therapists but did not stay in therapy for more than a couple of sessions. When I asked them the reason for discontinuing therapy they shared with me that they felt judged by those therapists who labeled them as "delinquents" with "psychopathic", "hysterical" or "narcissistic" personalities. These teenagers found that their therapists demanded that they follow the rules and regulations, which they resented and resisted. Within a short time these creative teenagers recreated a tense relationship with their therapists similar to the one they had with their parents, teachers and other authority figures. In many cases the tension escalated to the point that those teenagers stopped going back to see their therapists and the parents could not convince them to change their minds.

I feel fortunate that most of these creative teenagers connect with me and I am able to help them work through their conflicts and achieve success in their personal, family, educational and social lives. When I reflect upon all those creative young people that I worked with, I realize that they resisted following rules and regulations because they did not respect authority. They consider all forms of authority to be what Einstein called "false authority", an authority that generates fear rather than respect in them and they feel intimidated rather than protected by their authority figures. Thus they react strongly against them. Their teachers and parents perceive their resentment and call them rebels and react in a punitive way.

It has been my observation that creative teenagers are comfortable with the nurturing parent but have great difficulty with the disciplinarian parent with whom they get into a power struggle. I find it interesting that in most traditional families mothers become the nurturing parent and fathers the disciplinarian parent, while in some modern families we see the reverse. In single parent families, the same parent has to play both roles. I met many mothers of Creative Children who had a wonderful relationship with their child as long as they were nurturing but the moment they became the disciplinarian, the child became resistive and they got into a power struggle. The situation becomes more complicated in blended families where the nurturing and disciplinarian roles need to be worked out more carefully between parents and children.

The conflicts between the creative teenager and the disciplinarian parent can easily create tension that can escalate to resentment and finally there is an angry and violent exchange, after which the teenager either runs away from home, gets kicked out or the police are called to take the teenager to a hospital or a shelter. The Children's Aid Society may be requested to find them a suitable foster home and then the power struggle starts all over again.

When I meet one of these teenagers, I attempt to connect with their creative side in a nurturing way. Rather than focusing on their anxiety, depression and anger and discussing their diagnosis, I inquire about their hobbies, passions and dreams. I ask what they read, write, play, paint, draw or sculpt, and I ask them

Creative Minority: Dreams and Dilemmas

to bring their creative products to show me. They are thrilled. Sometimes in their entire lives, I was the first one who showed such a keen interest in their creative interests.

Their parents are pleasantly surprised to see their teenage sons and daughters looking forward to their therapy sessions. After I develop a special bond with those teenagers and earn their trust, I ask them a simple but profound question, "Would you like to live a healthy, happy and successful life?" They usually say, "Yes." It is at that stage I share with them that I have named my clinic the Creative Psychotherapy Clinic because I feel that developing the creative side of our personality is intimately connected with our mental health. I share with them that I have come the conclusion as a therapist and a writer that for artists to be successful they have to be free and for artistic freedom they need financial and emotional independence. Like other people, artists need money to survive and buy their art supplies and have fun with their friends. During my honest and open discussions I ask them to draw a map of their lives highlighting their past, present and future. I ask them to plan how they can achieve economic and emotional independence.

Once those creative teenagers are connected with me and are motivated to change I help them
- find part time jobs
- go back to school
- negotiate realistic expectations from their family
- find a place to live and
- develop a circle of friends, that I call their Family of the Heart, who are supportive and appreciative of their creative life.

Dr. K. Sohail

I also work with parents, suggesting that they not ask for rent money so that those teenagers feel appreciated. I ask parents to acknowledge their progress and steps to independence.

After the financial independence, I encourage emotional independence and discuss their romantic lives. I share with them that creative people need to be with special partners who can accept their need to be on their own and have private time to do their creative work and not feel rejected and abandoned. I invite their partners and have open and honest discussion about their mutual expectations. The issues become more complicated if these creative teenagers are pregnant or have children. We have discussions about balancing creative and family lives. I suggest to teenagers who are contemplating marriage and family life that they wait till they mature enough to take on that responsibility. I share with them that having a family is one of the most important decisions for creative people. I have met many artists who regretted taking that step. They adore their children but sometimes wish they never had them, as they are so involved in their creative work that they do not have time to fulfill their parental responsibilities. The choice of having children can be difficult for average people but can become far more difficult for creative people. I ask teenagers to take that choice very seriously and not commit to the responsibilities of family life until they are ready for them.

With this type of support and discussion, creative teenagers and young adults can start to feel better within a few months. As they improve, their anxiety and depression and anger subside, and they develop a healthier relationship with authority figures. As the suffering decreases, they are able to discover a new balance between their personal and family, creative and social, artistic and romantic lives.

Once those teenagers accept their Creative Personalities, they can deal with the dilemmas associated with such a personality and lifestyle and develop a realistic plan to fulfill their dreams. Once families accept their creative teenagers they communicate better with them, resolve conflicts effectively and have realistic expectations.

Creative people need to become aware of their options and then make wise choices. Often they find their creative lives in conflict with their educational, professional and family lives. Creative people not only need to learn to nurture their creativity but also must come to terms with other aspects of their lives. Creativity, like love and spirituality, asks for sacrifices. Some artists are more ready to make sacrifices than others.

Sometimes I share aspects of my creative journey with these very special people. Most teenagers connect very well with my personal stories. I encourage them to read the biographies of Virginia Woolf, Vincent Van Gogh creative people in my book Virginia Woolf, Vincent Van Gogh, Diane Arbus, Ezra Pound, Anais Nin and many others. Those biographies help my patients to have realistic expectations of life.

Working with creative people can be more frustrating but also more rewarding than working with traditional people. I look forward to working with them and their families, as I learn as much from them as they learn from me.

Creative Minority: Dreams and Dilemmas

CHAPTER FIFTEEN

CREATIVE ADULTS AND PSYCHOTHERAPY ~ THE STORY OF ALICIA JONES

I remember the afternoon when I received a phone call from Dr. Gaal, a well respected family physician of our community. Dr. Gaal wanted me to accept Alicia for psychotherapy. She stated that Alicia was an extra-ordinary and unique person and I would enjoy working with her.

When Alicia came to see me, she wore black from head to toe. Her hair was black, her dress was black, even her shoes were black. She wore chains around her neck. She was dressed in the Goth style but with a touch of class.

During her initial interview she seemed shy and nervous. I tried to reassure her. She shared with me that she had been diagnosed with Manic Depressive illness and had been treated with lithium, antidepressants and supportive therapy for a number of years. She had a lot of regard for Dr. Gaal but Dr. Gaal had told her that she needed more help than her clinic could offer her. Since Alicia respected Dr. Gaal she was willing to work with me.

When I met Alicia, she was living with her parents and her sister and had not been working for a number of years. As I got to know her, I discovered that Alicia had a keen interest in poetry, music, painting and sculpting. She also loved animals and had a number of them in her room in the basement of her house. It did not take me long to realize that she had a Creative Personality.

I was lucky that Alicia felt comfortable and connected with me and we could work together. I asked her to bring me a poem that would reflect her existential dilemma. Many writers express themselves better and share more of themselves on paper than verbally. Alicia brought the following poem for me.

THE WOMAN IN
THE CLAW FOOT BATHTUB
The room is filled with steam
There is a tangy smell in the suffocating air
I see the claw foot bathtub
The overhead shower is running
Behind the pale shower curtain I see a form slumped over
The tangy sweet smell grows sharper as I approach the claw shaped bathtub
I slowly lean forward
My fingers grasping the shower curtain
My heart pounding
The heat is intolerable as I struggle to breathe another breath
Slowly I pull the curtain back
Her head lay to the side with her hair plastering her face
The hot needles of water hit her white flesh
Her face frozen in hopeless sorrow
I stare at her safely
She looks like a life size naked doll
Black makeup runs like murky tears down her hollow cheeks
I see the bluish bruising on her breasts, her legs and her face
Seeming as though she were in battle with something and

lost
Her thin scarred arms lay by her side
Her wrists facing upwards
Towards a heaven that will never accept her, she will never know
The red waters swirl as her blood runs off her fingertips
The gashes on each wrist appear savagely open
Spilling her life down the drain
I stand over her frozen in place with horror
The claw foot bathtub is stained red
The blood runs down her lips and off her chin
Her nose bleeds giving her lips a scarlet tinge
Her fingernails hold blood clots
I continue to stare at the woman in the claw foot bathtub
Until I realize I AM the woman in the claw foot bathtub

Alicia's poem made me wonder whether she was abused in the past and could not share the details in her therapy sessions. I also realized that she struggled with self destructive and suicidal ideas.

After Alicia shared that poem, it was not uncommon for her to bring to the session a page with a poem or an entry of her diary. Gradually her creative writing became an integral part of her therapy to deal with her Creative Personality.

When Alicia had developed a trusting therapeutic relationship with me, I invited her parents to a session. They were kind and gentle but quite traditional. They had no understanding of Alicia's personality. They just knew that they had one normal daughter and one abnormal daughter who suffered from emotional problems and mental illness and they were willing to support her in any way they could, as they loved her.

When I shared with them that their daughter Alicia had a Creative Personality, they said they had never heard of that expression. When I explained to

Dr. K. Sohail

them that people with Creative Personality:
- are highly emotionally sensitive
- do not like to follow rules
- exhibit unconventional thinking
- follow non-traditional lifestyles
- like to express their creative talent and
- want to be unique in every possible way, they agreed that Alicia had all those characteristics.

When I shared with them that one day she would be able to live on her own and would become economically and emotionally independent, they said it would be a miracle. I smiled and confidently stated that creative people are able to perform miracles with proper support and guidance. During that interview I discovered that Alicia's loving father had prepared himself to support his mentally ill daughter all his life.

After a few months of therapy Alicia's parents told me that they were planning to retire and move close to their extended family in the Maritimes. Alicia was contemplating moving with them. I suggested to her that she stay back and learn to live independently without her parents. She reluctantly agreed. I referred her to the Canadian Mental Health Association who helped her find a place where she could live with her animals. She was thrilled. Her parents helped her settle in. That was a major breakthrough in therapy. Within a few months Alicia felt comfortable in her new place and started enjoying her privacy and independence. Her parents felt reassured. They could not believe that they were moving away without having to worry about Alicia.

As Alicia loved animals, I focused in therapy on her relationship with them. For her they were like her friends and children. She had adopted many of them as they were homeless and had looked after them till they died. She was a local Mother Teresa of animals who did not like to see animals suffering and dying in pain. She tried to reduce and heal their suffering the best she could. Animals brought out the best in her and I used her compassion for animals as a powerful factor in her healing. One day she brought the following poem, reflecting her feelings about her adopted guinea pig.

POE

When I first saw you
You were sad and alone
With no place to call home
No one to love you
No one who cared
You sat day in and day out
An outcast
Disfigured and lonely
My heart went out to you
So you came home with me
You had anew beginning in life
Our battles were many
But all held love within them
You quickly became a very important thing in my life
Your anger and frustration
I understood completely
The abuse you suffered had scarred you deeply
So I made it a goal to soothe your pain
Never once did I ever feel like giving up on you
For I wanted you to trust me
I needed you to finally let your guard down
To know that no one would ever hurt you again
You entered my heart
And it took years
But I knew you loved me too
You were just unable to show it as easily
That has never mattered
I have and will always love you my precious Poe

Dr. K. Sohail

You have been the leader when the rest stayed confused
So fearless and outspoken
You have been placed on a special pedestal
So as you've grown older
And begin to fade away
I hope I have treated you the best I could
I hope you may die happy
Knowing that you are loved
And that you will forever remain in a special place in my heart
Poe, there will never be another, my precious Poe

Keeping Alicia's love for animals in mind, I suggested to her that she might do some volunteer work with local humane society. She readily agreed. Within a few weeks she not only made new friends, she also impressed the staff with her dedication and commitment to the welfare of animals.

As therapy progressed her depression improved, she stopped cutting herself, made new friends and took steps towards emotionally stability and independence.

The second breakthrough happened in therapy when Alicia was offered a part time job at the humane society. Alicia was ecstatic. That was a major step towards her economic independence.

The last time Alicia's mother visited Ontario, she came to see me and thanked me for helping her daughter. I acknowledged her unconditional love and support for her daughter.

There were moments in therapy when Alicia became angry with me as I gently pushed her towards health and independence. I let her express her feelings but remained firm. Gradually she realized that I was there to help her, not hurt her. Now that she has healed she is able to appreciate the "tough love" she received from me. Now we can laugh and joke about those tense moments when we challenged each other and finally found creative ways to resolve our conflicts.

In the last couple of years Alicia has learnt to accept her Creative Personality, make new friends and lead an emotionally and economically independent life. Her parents and her doctor are quite impressed by her progress. So am I. She is far more emotionally stable, productive and peaceful than when I first met her. When I shared with her that I am working on a creative psychotherapy project highlighting the issues of psychotherapy with creative people and asked her if she would like to contribute, she readily agreed to share her story. We chose the pseudonym Alicia Jones to respect her privacy. She shared the story of her struggles in these words.

ALICIA JONES' STORY

When I think back about how my life has been I'm often surprised that I'm still alive. So many times I've been at death's door pounding and screaming to be let in. But there is someone that pleads with my soul not to give up. When I was younger, like so many others, I wanted to fit in. But I was betrayed by people I loved. I did not know manic depression was waiting for me to break, which I did, and it leaked into my body like toxic waste.

So at twelve years of age, I was already falling to the bottom. It's just puberty my mom told me. But was it supposed to affect my mind the way it did. I remember taking large doses of Anacin number 3 and Tylenol number 3 for splitting headaches. Not knowing yet that they were migraines. My sister was my closest best friend till I was 14. We created story lines and plots with our 100 Barbie dolls. Hours were spent making up soap opera scenes where nobody was singled out and every one had good husbands and boyfriends. Even though we were short on Ken dolls all the women were happy and beautiful. This was the fantasy life we wanted. Julie matured, had friends, boyfriends, popularity, and is still the life of every party.

Well I tried, but I could not come out of my shell. I was extremely shy, hiding behind my long blonde hair. I never felt good enough or pretty enough. People took advantage of my trust and kindness. Having parents from Nova Scotia, we were taught respect for others, not to judge and see the good in everyone. If you said you'd do something, you kept your promise. My mom wanted us to treat others the way we would like to be treated by others. But people in Ontario don't care as much as people do down East. I learnt the hard way.

When I entered high school, my true hell began. I was terrorized by other girls, for reasons I still don't understand. I was so shy that I didn't talk to people. Maybe that made me different. I was to find out later that my silence unnerved these girls. They thought I was a bitch too good to talk to them. But I was really afraid to speak. Gradually I fell into myself and music. I listened to special groups. Finally Tool entered my life and Maynard was awakened in my brain. I knew by late grade nine that I was very different from others. My morbid thoughts began to come out in my clothes and make up. In grade ten I got into a group of skinheads who abused me both mentally and physically. They degraded me and basically destroyed what was left of my self-esteem. They made me feel that I needed them, and I would be nothing without them. And I believed that for a long time. I lost my virginity at 15 and I felt nothing.

I was put on Prozac which helped me a little. My headaches increased. I started doing drugs to numb myself. But I wasn't numb enough after I was raped at 16. After that I began cutting myself and took overdoses many times only to throw up or get stitches. Maynard was becoming more dominant in my mind and my life. I went to listen to his band live and for what felt an eternity he made eye contact with me. That is when I felt him take my soul and place a part of him into me. Instead of crying I was finally angry. I knew that I did not deserve what these skinheads did to me. When I was 17 I was put on Lithium. By now I was completely manic-depressive. The cutting increased. My hatred for men and school increased. I started not caring who I slept with. I did a lot of drugs and drank. I had a boyfriend who I thought loved me. But one day he forced himself on me saying over and over again "I am raping you." So things went downhill after that.

In 1996 I tried to move out but failed. All of my art became angry and portrayed rape scenes. I held in my secrets of misery from my mom until one day after a fight I screamed it all out to her. She was devastated. It was getting to a point now where I would have violent outbursts. My sister feared me. I was a monster. I hated everyone but most of all I hated myself. But part of me cried out to live a normal life. I fell head over heels in love with "Lucas."

I had been to various therapists and doctors. I was a guinea pig to a number of horrible drugs. It pushed me to the brink of suicide and back. Lucas played my illness to his advantage. I knew his father suffered from manic depression so I thought I found a perfectly understanding boyfriend. But I was the one who did everything for him. But he believed everything that went wrong was my fault because I was "fucked up", "crazy" "'psycho." I was completely unstable. My self-mutilation was peaking. I had 160-200 cuts on each arm. I used to cut my breasts and stomach. All I wanted was to cut out the pain. But I could never bleed out all the bad and was getting stitched up. One night I overdosed on acid, pain killers, weed and booze. My friends told me I stopped breathing and doctors had to give me CPR to save my life. I felt Maynard becoming more and more aggressive in my mind. Finally I realized this had to stop. Loving Lucas was killing me. I realized I was betrayed by people I once loved. I did not belong anywhere. I wanted to die. Lucas and I broke up and my life was nothing but a *depressed bloody mess.*

Dr. Gaal finally sent me to the Creative Psychotherapy Clinic, where I got the right therapy. I had been to other therapists but nothing had worked. But I gave it one more try. I allowed myself to trust a male doctor. It has been hard, very hard, but now I have my own place and a job after five years of unemployment. If I didn't have my animals and my ability to write I know my sanity would be gone. Now everyone in my family says that I'm the strongest woman of all of us. To me it is a choice, either you fight or you kill yourself. I don't care what other people think. I am going to dress the way I want, think the way I want and be myself. Finally I reached a stage where I can be painfully honest and to the point. I know I will never be "normal" but I do not wish to be. It took me a long time to accept the way I think and feel. And I know now that the only way I can learn things is the hard way. It is the price you pay for being creative.

CHAPTER SIXTEEN

LACKING INNER DISCIPLINE, STRUCTURE AND ORGANIZATION

I was always fascinated by the people in my clinical practice who were intelligent, bright and very effective in their career but still struggled in their work life. Some became unsuccessful and unhappy but did not know the reason why. Many had seen a number of doctors and therapists. They shared with me that they had received a number of diagnoses including psychopathic and narcissistic personality disorders, which bothered them.

After my assessment, when they asked my opinion I told them that they had a creative personality and because of their unconventional thinking and non-traditional lifestyle, they experienced problems in their life. Since they had a well-developed *creative self* they were successful in doing what they liked and loved to do but because they had a poor *conditioned self*, they had difficulties following rules and becoming part of institutions. Some lacked inner discipline and structure and needed external help to become a part of the organization in which they worked.

If such people remained single, they learned to

- 139 -

accept their disorganized lifestyle, but when they got married and had children; their families had difficulties dealing with them. They found them engaging and frustrating at the same time. Because of their intelligence and creativity, the spouses and children found them exciting, but because they lacked inner discipline and did not fulfill their promises, their families also found them frustrating.

After establishing a good connection with such people in therapy, I made them aware of their limitations as well as their strengths and asked them to get help from others to follow the rules and fulfill their promises.

One such person was Bruce. He was an excellent lawyer and did well in court but had great difficulties keeping record of his services and sending invoices. Although people owed him thousands of dollars, his wife struggled with paying bills. She was so frustrated that she was contemplating leaving him. She took him to see a number of therapists but they could not help him. When Bruce and his wife met me I told them that a few months of therapy would control his problem. She was quite skeptical. As I worked with him I asked her to stop judging and criticizing him and let me make him aware of his deficiency.

After a few weeks of therapy, I started giving him homework, which he followed. At one stage I asked him to make a list of the money owed to him and send invoices out to his clients. Within a few days he received more than fifty thousand dollars. He not only paid his debts but also took his family on a vacation. That was a major step in the improvement of his relationship with his wife and family. After Bruce realized his problem he started designating work to his staff and asked their help to stay on top of things.

At one stage, I asked Bruce if he would be kind

Creative Minority: Dreams and Dilemmas

enough to share his experiences in therapy so that others could learn from his story. I was confident that his answers would help many to review their lives and work. He readily agreed, but even after making a commitment he took the longest to complete the questionnaire. He was the last one to send me his story for this book. It did not frustrate me as I knew his interview was worth waiting for.

Green, Yellow and Red Zones

THE GREEN ZONE
When people choose to live in the Green Zone they are, amongst many other things, pleasant and cheerful. They easily carry on a rational discussion with those around them and, should a difference of opinion arise, they are able to enthusiastically connect with a healthy and constructive inner strength that will encourage the dialogue that helps to resolve or dissolve their conflicts – and most importantly - build bridges that span all differences.

THE YELLOW ZONE
When in the Yellow Zone people feel somewhat distressed. Anxiety, sadness and anger too often rule their thoughts and actions. Because of their discomfort, they are unable to communicate with others effectively and are poorly equipped to deal with stressful situations or interpersonal conflicts. This Zone is a slippery slope that often leads to many problems that await them when they cannot hold on and fall into the Red Zone.

THE RED ZONE
Those who occupy the Red Zone are extremely unhappy, emotionally exhausted, usually maintain a

high state of hidden anger and are extremely distressed. They often lose control and become abusive or completely withdrawn from others, sometimes fleeing to escape — even from themselves! They have great difficulty dealing with stressful situations, unable to have a rational discussion to resolve or dissolve their interpersonal conflicts. At times they lack the will to take care of their personal appearance, overlook proper nourishment and avoid being responsible for family members in their charge.

Interview

1. Which one of the three Zones were you working in when you first came to see me?

   Response:
   When I first came to see you in December 2001, I was working almost exclusively in the Red Zone with occasional forays into the Yellow. I did spend some time in the Green. This would occur shortly after the commencement of submissions and argument in Court. I would get a natural high or rush from litigation and during these times there would be nothing else in my mind or my life but the intense focus on the judge and other lawyer, as well as the joy of a good argument or cross examination of a witness. Other than those brief periods in Court, I was pretty miserable all the time.

2. What symptoms were evident in your day-to-day life?

Response:

I was very stressed and unhappy for most of my working hours (not to mention non-working hours). I had a very full practice with some great clients and challenging, enjoyable files. I spent many hours at work, probably close to 100 per week. The legal work that I did was very good, at times brilliant, and those clients would be extremely pleased and had no trouble recommending me to others. Indeed, my practice has been built exclusively by word of mouth, I have never advertised or promoted in any way.

However, I was unable to consistently complete any of the practical, easy or mundane aspects of private practice. The docketing of my billable hours was inconsistent and incomplete which always made billing, when it happened, a very time consuming, difficult and frustrating chore. As a result, the income in no way reflected the amount or quality of work and my debt load just kept increasing. Moreover, there was work-in-process strewn all over my office. Files would often be taken to a certain point and then not finished (which also contributed to billing problems). There was no organization and very little planning or follow-up, which always left me on the verge of missing something crucial and potentially facing a negligence suit.

3. How was this affecting your personal and family lives?

Response:

Dr. K. Sohail

Working the extremely long hours meant that I rarely saw my family. I left before my wife and children were awake and came home after they were asleep. My first wife left (with the kids) and my second wife had become completely baffled and estranged. I had missed out on so much of my children's lives and I really had next to nothing to show for it.

4. How long were you struggling with those problems?

    Response:
    Upon reflection, I can see now that I have struggled with this problem my whole life. My academic career had been a continuous series of incomplete assignments, last minute cramming and mediocre results interspersed with occasional brilliance. I have credits from four universities but did not get a degree (law is my only degree) until I was 40. I have held many different jobs in a very wide range of fields and have been almost universally fired from each one.

5. What did other doctors / therapists suggest as diagnoses and treatment?
    Response:
    From my perspective, Ontario is a horrible place to seek help with mental health issues. There seems to be a real shortage of practitioners and it is next to impossible to find one person or organization who is able and willing to dispense drugs and provide counseling or therapy. Before seeing you, I was diagnosed with a number of personality

disorders and other emotional conditions including Narcissism, Anti-social Personality, Depression, Anxiety Disorder and Attention Deficit Disorder. There were others, but I can no longer recall what they were. Treatments included drugs such as Paxil, Effexor, Dexedrine, Ritalin, Prozac and cocktail-like combinations of the above. For those who are not doctors or patients, I was taking anti-depressants, stimulants and anti-anxiety drugs at various times. The only therapy or counseling available was privately offered through psychologists but not on any kind of regular or consistent basis. It was all quite ineffective.

6. How did therapy at our clinic help you?

Response:
You told me right from the beginning that there would be no labels because no one fits neatly into any so-called "disorder" (although I suspect that a standard analysis was made for OHIP and file purposes). You approached my treatment by determining the practical and day-to-day effects of my problem and not spending months trying to find out what trauma in my infancy have caused it. So long as the problem is identified, and the patient takes ownership of it, you assist in the treatment by helping to create a long term plan for dealing with it and provide practical advice on dealing with specific, personal issues. There is plenty of encouragement and feedback. The weekly sessions establish and review what you call baby steps which are a

breakdown of the longer range plan into small, relatively easily achievable steps towards correcting the problem. As well, after more than a year of dealing with the negative side effects (and lack of positive effects) of many drugs, I was pleased to learn that you resorted to medications only as a last option.

7. How did you learn to live in the Green Zone and not be affected by other people's moods when they are in their Yellow or Red Zone?

Response:
Through speaking with you, I came to the realization after about five or six months that the only person I can control is me. My wife had been reacting quite badly to my problems and as a result, was very moody, depressed and withdrawn. Unwittingly, I had been letting her feelings infect me, which not only made me miserable all the time but also interfered with my attempts to correct my problems. You helped me to develop what you call an "emotional raincoat" to deflect the moods of others and let me concentrate on making me better, letting me live in my Green Zone despite what others were feeling.

8. When did you realize that you lacked the inner discipline, structure and organization in spite of being a very intelligent and creative person?

Response:
After about 9 months of therapy, I came to accept that there was something actually

missing inside me that could not be overcome merely by force of will or practice. I know that I am intelligent and that I am capable of great creativity, but I don't have any self discipline, self organization or any kind of internal structure with which I can meet the demands of my law practice and the daily requirements of being a good husband and father.

9. When did you realize that you needed help from your colleagues if you were to be successful in your professional life?

Response:
Once I came to the acceptance that I don't have the necessary internal structure, I concluded (with your gentle prodding) that the structure must be built externally. My father once told me that the only thing I needed was to hire someone to follow me around and record everything I do, which would take care of the docketing and let others have the necessary information to do all the billing. As it turns out, he was not far off the mark, although I scoffed at the time. I have had to, and am in the process of assembling a team of people (so far parts of three clerks, a secretary and a junior lawyer) to create the structure, organization and discipline which I lack internally.

For mental health professionals, it is interesting to note that creative personalities that do not exist in the classification of personality disorders do have some characteristics that they share with narcissistic and anti-social personalities, but there are also significant differences. Narcissistic and anti-social personalities have a bad conscience as they are manipulative, selfish and sometimes exploitative. They do not have any sense of remorse or guilt after they hurt the people dear to them. On the other hand, creative personalities have a good conscience and they genuinely care for others, especially their families and friends. They hurt others because of their laziness and carefreeness and feel guilty afterwards. Their dear ones see them as careless rather than carefree, impulsive rather than spontaneous and irresponsible rather than free-spirited. In my clinical practice, I invite spouses, relatives and close friends of such people and explain the condition to them. After they understand the dynamics they are better able to cope with them. Creative people are so pre-occupied with the things they love to do that they become oblivious to other people's needs.

When those creative people understand the dynamics of their problem and realize that their creative personality is a mixed blessing, they are able to reorganize their lives and become more productive and successful. They need other caring people in their lives to support them. I believe that the strength of secretaries and assistants is that they can organize and coordinate the work lives of those individuals who are very creative but disorganized. I think it is unfortunate that because we do not have any room for creative personalities in our classifications, we label them as psychopaths, which is a big blow to

Creative Minority: Dreams and Dilemmas

their self image and creates a crisis for them and their dear ones. I am not suggesting that there are no psychopaths who can be creative; I am suggesting that we need to differentiate them from those creative people who are not psychopaths.

My special interest in creative personalities and their emotional and social problems led me to interview dozens of writers in my literary career.

Creative Minority: Dreams and Dilemmas

CHAPTER SEVENTEEN

DREAMS CHANGE
- by
JL

With my guitar hanging off my shoulder, I smiled into the bright stage lights. This was everything my 16-year-old heart could want. From that moment on, I knew how I wanted my life to go; concerts, tours and life on the road. I fought for that dream at every gig and every band practice. It wasn't until I saw myself on video that reality hit me hard-I definitely did not have the talent to make it in the music business. It was a bitter pill, but I swallowed it.

Still in love with the music industry and its glamour, I shifted gears and tried to find a niche for myself. Having always loved writing, I decided to pursue a career in music journalism. I earned my Bachelors of Arts degree in English with a minor in journalism and got a reporting job at a weekly newspaper. I interviewed bands and wrote about them every chance I got. It was definite; I wanted to be an entertainment journalist and travel the country interviewing famous rock stars. To give myself an edge over the competition, I earned a Master of Arts degree in Journalism and then moved to the big city. My dream job was almost within reach, when a popular music magazine offered me an interview. The interview went well and the publisher told me that he liked me and as far as he was concerned, I had the job.

Dr. K. Sohail

I was in Heaven, then reality crashed in - the editor liked my work but wanted someone with more experience. I was devastated and ended up selling doggie raincoats and other pet products in a pet boutique. During this time, I wrote a Young Adults' novel. Although the novel ended up on a shelf, I discovered a love for writing novels which renewed my desire to find another writing job.

Finally, I found a writing job at another weekly newspaper and things looked good until I found out that I was to cover the local Board of Education and City Council beats. The job bored the hell out of me and I got even more depressed. When I thought things couldn't get any worse; I got fired from that job. My self-esteem landed in the toilet and my depression went into overdrive. I ended up in a day treatment program and was hospitalized three times because of my suicidal ideation.

"Suicidal Ideation" sounds so neat and clinical when the reality was: I was hurting bad enough to want to die just to escape my pain. I couldn't even look at myself in the mirror because I hated the "loser" that I'd become. Through the pain, I wrote an 80-page poetry book.

After my third hospitalization which resulted in my entering a long term psychotherapy program, I tried, with the help of my husband, to put the shattered remains of my life back together. I started writing a fiction novel loosely based on my experiences on the psych ward. I realized how much I still loved writing. It took me four years to write my novel during which time, I tried to move on and have a family.

Today, over 20 years since I stood on the stage, I'm still in love with music, but now I just listen to it instead of making it. I'm still writing though; I have to,

Creative Minority: Dreams and Dilemmas

it's like breathing. I just finished writing a children's picture book, and have started work on a young adult's novel and a thriller novel. When I'm not writing, I'm taking care of my children and puppy. I haven't had any of my books published yet, but I'm still trying. I refuse to give up on them. Writing carried me through the darkest times in my life; it was my life preserver when I was drowning in depression.

Creative Minority: Dreams and Dilemmas

Chapter Eighteen

PERSONALITY QUESTIONNAIRE

The following questionnaire has been devised to help you understand the creative and traditional elements in your personality.

To complete it, rate your response to each question from 0 (No) to 4 (Yes) then write it in the box after the question. Any number from 0 – 4 can be used to reflect your answer. Finally add your scores to get the total and refer to the end of the Questionnaire to learn what you score means.

#	Question	Score
1.	Have you been highly sensitive to sensory stimuli, for example, heat, cold and loud noises, since childhood?	
2.	Have you always had difficulties accepting authority?	
3.	Do you enjoy spending time with yourself and daydreaming?	
4.	Do you provoke strong emotional reactions in others?	
5.	Are you fascinated with beauty and aesthetics in shapes, colours, sounds or words?	
6.	Do you have a higher awareness of your	

	physical, emotional or social environment than people around you?	
7.	Do you have a broader range of empathy with people and animals than other people have?	
8.	Are you more fascinated with abstractions than concrete realities?	
9.	Do you have a strong need for creative expression and communication?	
10.	Do you believe you are passionate, strong-willed, and sometimes even stubborn?	
11.	Do you experience conflict with traditional organizations and systems?	
12.	Do you like to lead rather than follow?	
13.	Do you think unconventionally?	
14.	Do you have a non-traditional lifestyle?	
15.	Are you less concerned about money, time and cleanliness than your friends?	
16.	Do you disregard moral values of your community for which you have no respect?	
17.	Do you feel you have a strong dark side to your personality? For example, do people consider you selfish, egotistical, arrogant or brutally honest?	
18.	Do you rely more on your own experiences than on those of others?	
19.	Do you become easily bored with routine activities?	
21.	Do you feel you are vulnerable to having emotional problems and conflicts?	
22.	Is there a history of emotional problems/mental illness in your family?	

Creative Minority: Dreams and Dilemmas

23.	Are there writers, musicians, philosophers or artists (successful or frustrated) in your family?	
24.	Do you feel a desire or a need to improve the world?	
25.	Are you fascinated with the mysteries of life?	
	TOTAL SCORE	/100

SCORE 1-50

You have a traditional personality or you choose to live a traditional personal lifestyle, by following the rules and accepting authority. You prefer a peaceful stable lifestyle rather than an adventurous but risky lifestyle.

SCORE 51-75

You have a lot of creative potential. If you are in conflict between your traditional and creative self, you might need to review your lifestyle and resolve or dissolve your conflicts.

SCORE 76-100

You definitely have a creative personality. If you have accepted yourself and developed your creative potential, you might be very happy with the rewards of your efforts. But you might be in serious conflict with your family and community. If you have a family history of mental illness and you are suffering from emotional problems, you might consider seeing a psychotherapist to find a healthy balance and harmony in you life through new ways of channeling your creative energies.

Creative Minority: Dreams and Dilemmas

Chapter Nineteen

TRADITIONAL MAJORITY CREATIVE MINORITY

As a student of human psychology and a practicing psychotherapist I have developed a keen interest in the evolution of human mind in our personal and collective lives. Over the decades a number of psychologists have presented a number of interesting and fascinating theories about human personality. Based on my own professional and social experiences I have also been developing a theory of Traditional and Creative Personalities. In this essay I will share some of my concepts.

NATURAL SELF
All children are born with their unique temperament and special gift that can be called their Natural Self. It is similar to the seed of the plant. Like a seed needs fertile soil, ample sunshine and fresh air to grow and become a healthy tree and bear fruits, human children also need loving, caring and compassionate homes, schools and communities to become healthy and happy, loving and peaceful adults. Those children who are exposed to neglect, abuse and violence turn into angry, bitter and violent adults that can become danger to themselves and to their communities.

CONDITIONED AND CREATIVE SELF

By the time children become teenagers their Natural Self has transformed into two distinct selves:

A. Conditioned Self

It is the outcome of the social and cultural conditioning of their families and schools, communities and cultures. Conditioned Self is guided by *should, have to and must.*

B. Creative Self

It is the expression of the creative dimension of the personality and is guided by what people *like to, want to and love to do.*

TRADITIONAL AND CREATIVE PERSONALITIES

Human personalities can be seen on a broad spectrum. On one end of the spectrum are people with Traditional Personalities who have well developed Conditioned Self and on the other end of the spectrum are people who have Creative Personalities who have well developed Creative Self. While many healthy, happy and peaceful people have discovered a balance between their Creative and Conditioned Self, there are others who are in conflict. Such a conflict can lead to anxiety, shame, guilt and depression, even breakdown. It happens when Creative Self wants to do those things that Conditioned Self considers wrong, bad and sinful.

THREE SOURCES OF SOCIAL CONDITIONING

For the students of human psychology the questions arise:

What is right and what is wrong?

What is good and what is bad?

Creative Minority: Dreams and Dilemmas

What is a sin and what is a virtue?
When we study different communities and cultures we realize that the values of right and wrong, good and bad and sin and virtue can come from three traditions.

A. RELIGIOUS TRADITION
Some cultures have a strong religious tradition and people believe in Gods, prophets, scriptures and religious leaders. Those religious leaders, whether priests or pundats, maulanas or rabbis, tell people what they should or should not do and if they do what they should not be doing then they would be committing a sin for which they would be punished in this world and the world hereafter. When religious people do not follow the dictates of their scriptures they feel guilty. In such cultures the authority of right and wrong rests with heavenly Gods and scriptures.

B. LEGAL TRADITION
Those cultures that are secular have a legal tradition. They have constitutions that have laws for their citizens. Those laws guide people what they should or should not do. Those people who break those laws are considered criminals, tried in courts and sent to jail. In secular cultures the authority of deciding right and wrong lies with humans not Gods

C. HEALTH TRADITION
Some cultures that are health conscious have social traditions that are guided by doctors and nurses, psychologists and psychiatrists, scientists and health care experts. These professionals share their observations and results of their scientific experiments and research to guide people to adopt principles of healthy living. Those guidelines help people what they

Dr. K. Sohail

should or should not do to remain physically and mentally healthy. If people would not follow those guidelines they would get ill and sick and suffer.

In most communities in the world cultural traditions are a mixture of religious, legal and health traditions that evolve with time.

TRADITIONAL MAJORITY / CREATIVE MINORITY

When we study human civilization we realize that in every community and culture there is a majority of traditional people and a minority of creative people. People with Traditional Personalities like to follow the rules and love to protect organizations and institutions whether social or cultural, religious or political. On the other hand people with Creative Personalities challenge authority. They like to break the rules they find irrational and unjust and challenge organizations and institutions they find restrictive and suffocating. Interestingly enough if we follow the evolution of any culture we will find that the creative minority of one century grows into the traditional majority of the next century and gives birth to a new creative minority who leads humanity to the next stage of evolution. It is fascinating to see how the villains of one generation become the heroes of the next generation.

BIOGRAPHIES OF CREATIVE PERSONALITIES

When we study the biographies of Creative Personalities whether scientists or artists, poets or philosophers, reformers or revolutionaries, we find that they suffered because they were frequently in conflict with their traditional families, communities and cultures. It was not unusual for those traditional families and communities to appreciate the gifts and ideas of those creative people after a few decades, sometimes centuries, and shower them with rewards and awards. In the 20th century we saw a number of examples of that phenomenon. I will just share two such examples, one from the world of politics and the other from the worlds of science and religion.

Nelson Mandela of South Africa challenged the White Government and their racist laws and policies of apartheid. He was put in jail and declared a 'terrorist' but after spending a quarter of a century in jail he was released and seen as a 'freedom fighter'. He was awarded a Nobel Peace Prize for creating a multi-racial, multi-cultural democratic government in South Africa. The other example is of the Catholic Church that recognized the discoveries of Galileo, who was penalized and persecuted for three hundred years, because his findings about our universe were considered to be in conflict with the traditional and literal interpretations of the Bible.

In every community, Creative Personalities are trying to protect personal freedom. They believe that human beings have to be free to experience their creativity in their own unique way. Such creativity can be expressed in science as well as art, love as well as spirituality. Creative Personalities feel concerned that autocratic and restrictive religious and political institutions can kill the creative spark in people.

When we study different communities and cultures of the world, we can see that there are times in history when the traditional majority and creative minority are in conflict. Such conflict can lead to angry and bitter, even violent, confrontations. On the other hand there are times when the traditional majority and creative minority are in harmony and create a peaceful environment conducive for growth and evolution. That is the time when the creative minority appreciates that the traditional majority is securing and protecting the creative gifts of the past generations and the traditional majority appreciates that the creative minority is paving the way for future generations. It is a healthy balance between traditional majority and creative minority that is most productive and progressive. Such a balance is hard to achieve in families, communities and cultures but it is an ideal that we can strive to achieve.

CLOSED AND OPEN SYSTEMS

It is evident from history that when any system becomes a closed system and does not grow with time and does not flow like a river, then it becomes stagnant like a pond and loses its freshness. On the other hand when a system remains open and is practiced by progressive and open-minded people it continues to grow and evolve producing wonderful fruits of love and labor. Life moves forwards not backwards. In any community and culture different people, whether traditional or creative, can follow their dreams and find their respectable place in society but they need to respect the role of other people in creating a balanced life and community. With the passage of time we are realizing that human beings have unity in diversity and diversity in unity and such a realization is a key for future growth and evolution. I hope one day traditional majority and creative minority learn to respect and appreciate each other and work together for the common good of humanity. If humanity is like a boat then traditional majority is like an anchor and creative minority is like the sails. If humanity is like a tree then traditional majority is like the roots and creative minority is like branches and fruits. Throughout human history traditional majority has been representing our glorious past and creative minority has been an inspiration for our golden future.

Creative Minority: Dreams and Dilemmas

CHAPTER TWENTY

CREATIVE MINORITY

Creative people have always intrigued me
  I am fascinated by
    Minds of scientists
      Hearts of artists
       Souls of mystics
          Logic of philosophers
            Passion of reformers
              And
                  Rebellion of revolutionaries
                    They have all guided humanity
                      To the next stage of evolution
For years
   I have been trying to
      Understand their personalities
         Analyze their philosophies
         And
            Appreciate their contributions to history
               Creative people are always in minority
                 But they guide
                    The traditional majority to new heights
                      and
                          depths of life

       Sohail

Dr. Sohail's Books available on Amazon Kindle

Becoming a Psychotherapist

Prophets of Violence, Prophets of Peace

From Islam to Secular Humanism

Love, Sex and Marriage

The Art of Loving in your Green Zone

Green Zone Living: 7 Steps to a Happy, Healthy and Peaceful Lifestyle

The Myth of the Chosen One

Freedom of Religion, Freedom from Religion

The Art of Living in your Greenzone

The Art of Working in your Greenzone

Sexual Fantasies and Social Realities

Dr. K. Sohail

Creating Green Zone Schools

The Man Titanic left Behind

From Holy War to Global Peace

From Breakdowns to Breakthroughs

The Next Stage of Human Evolution

www.ingramcontent.com/pod-product-compliance
Lightning Source LLC
Chambersburg PA
CBHW021159010426
R18062100001B/R180621PG41931CBX00031B/55